The Purposeful Love of God

The Purposeful
Love of God

GOD'S LOVE FROM HIS PERSPECTIVE

By

WILLIAM J. LAURENCE

STRAIT ROAD PRESS

Edited by Kathlyn Jones
Cover Design by Nabin Karna
Cover Illustration by
Stanislav Agafonov (aka luvdraft)

This 2nd edition first published in 2025 by Strait Road Press
Mangonui, New Zealand. www.straitroadpress.com

ISBN 978-1-7385952-0-4

Copyright © 2025 by William J. Laurence

All rights reserved.

No part of this publication may be reproduced, distributed, or transmitted in any form or by any means, including photocopying, recording, or other electronic or mechanical methods, without the prior written permission of the publisher, except as permitted by U.S. copyright law. For permission requests, go to www.straitroadpress.com

Unless otherwise stated, all scripture quotations taken from the (NASB®) New American Standard Bible®, Copyright © 1995 by The Lockman Foundation. Used by permission. All rights reserved. lockman.org

ACKNOWLEDGEMENTS

There are many people who have helped me in bringing this little book to fruition. Some have put in a lot of hours and some a little, as they were able, but I am grateful to each one.

It was very helpful, especially in the early stages, to have a group of trusted friends and family, who I could rely upon to offer honest comment, and with whom I could gauge how well I was expressing ideas that have been percolating in my head for many years, but never written down until now.

I thank one of my daughters-in-law (an English teacher), who read and also helped edit the book, and patiently listened as I argued for the merits of my own archaic style.

I am particularly indebted to my three sons, who would often, on their own initiative, turn our casual conversations to what I was writing at the time, allowing me the luxury of fleshing out my ideas further. The hours spent talking over these ideas was a constant encouragement to see the project through, and it meant more to me than I can hope to express in just a few short sentences.

Lastly, I want the express my gratitude to my wife, who has shared with me, and endured with patience, the life of the struggling artisan; and has not seen my writing as merely a distraction, but as a priority in our lives together in the service of our Lord.

WILLIAM J. LAURENCE

τῷ ἀγαπήσαντί με καὶ παραδόντι
ἑαυτὸν ὑπὲρ ἐμοῦ

PREFACE

Someone once wrote that there is nothing new under the sun, and that of books, there is no end. It is a delicious irony that he had to write a new book to say it.

Perhaps, at the time, he was reading his way through one of those needlessly long academic books, stretching too small a thought over too many tiresome pages; so we mustn't take his words too seriously. Whatever the case, it is clear that he wrote those words in a mood of deep depression, and consequently gave to the world one of the most depressing books of all time.

There is a truth to his words of course, but it is only a small truth, and neglects the greater; and the author knew as much, even as he wrote and gave physical form to the thoughts in his head. His words do not admit of the thrill of seeing that same sun rising in a new light each and every day; or, with the wonder and joy of a child, experiencing a new and extraordinary thought, about something that just a minute before seemed so familiar and mundane.

So, if his words are to mean anything for us, they should be taken more as an admonition to read less, but

Preface

better books. Whether this is such a book the reader must judge, but I can say that it has been my joy to experience the wonder of seeing something new again in the writing of these pages; and my sincere hope that the reader may share in the same. In any case, if my thoughts are small to some, I have not, at least, stretched them out over too many pages.

❦

But I would be remiss if I did not say a word on behalf of those who have lead me here; the scholars and faithful theologians – many of whom have long since crossed over the river, while a few tarry still on this side – who have taught me the wonder and thrill of the gospel. This book could not have been written without their profound insight and dedicated labour, and if there is anything inspirational written in these pages, it can, in large part, be traced back to them.

For the student of God who may yet be unfamiliar with his name, I would especially like to mention P. T. Forsyth. It was he who lifted me from the smog of religious intellectualism, out into the rarefied air of heaven itself. He taught me more about God and His Christ than ever I cared to know of mere Christianity; and I would encourage every serious disciple to read his works.

However, this book does not come from academia,

though its tone is, perhaps, somewhat intellectual. Neither is its intention to impress with its theology or philosophy, though it touches on them both. Rather, it springs from the simple faith and life of someone who has made his living as a builder of fine stringed instruments – the life of an artisan.

I am content to let that stand as my qualification to write this book, for it is no exaggeration to say, that without that life, this book could not have been written.

That is not to disparage scholarship, or deny it its proper place, but the church has too often surrendered its responsibilities to the professional class, and has unwittingly created the impression that class is the sole repository for the knowledge of God. If that were true, it would not have pleased the Father to send His Son as a carpenter. I could mention other examples, of course, but none more striking. And is there anyone who thinks Christ's humble life and occupation were simply an unfortunate accident of history?

And grant that His occupation was deliberately chosen for Him by the Father. It is easy to assume it was selected simply to better contrast His former status in heaven, and to show there were no obstacles that the power of God could not overcome. But is it not possible that there was something latent, even active, in that humble occupation that made its choice a necessity?

For knowledge does not come by one path alone and though scholarship is vital, it is not exhaustive. There is

Preface

insight and wisdom that can only be gained from outside the professional class. We need both if we would gain a more mature understanding of our God. Paul, the tent maker, would agree with that – not to mention David, the shepherd king. And this book is written in that same tradition.

WILLIAM J. LAURENCE

Contents

Acknowledgements   V
Preface   VIII

CHAPTER I

Concerning Words   1

CHAPTER II

The Husband   17

CHAPTER III

The Father   29

CHAPTER IV

The Artisan   49
Part i

CHAPTER V

The Artisan   61
Part ii

CHAPTER VI
Steadfast Love   71

CHAPTER VII
Everlasting Love   81

CHAPTER VIII
The Beginning of God's Love   95

CHAPTER IX
The Return of the Bride   111

CHAPTER X
The Moral Imperative   127

CHAPTER I

Concerning Words

HE WRITTEN WORD captures the character of a culture at the time of writing, much like we can see, in an instant, the wind blowing wheat in a field. And a language might be likened to a wheat field – with each head of grain, a word – that ebbs and flows as the winds of culture blow over it.

Some words, like heads of wheat, are so closely entwined with each other that in the back and forth of daily life, they can cover almost the same ground. On occasion, the prevailing winds of culture can force them to bend, in one direction or another, for such a long time that their original character and meaning fades from living memory, along with the truth that meaning once conveyed.

But if words are living and pliable, they do not exist in and of themselves; their apparent freedom of movement belies the fact each word is connected, however flexibly, to the soil from which they came, and through which their life is sustained. That soil is the objective truth, the reality, that gives each word life, and however similar or confused they become, a distinction can still linger on – an echo from a long forgotten age.

However, if a word should be plucked from the soil, it will eventually die and truth can certainly be lost, though truth itself cannot die; it may be a generation, or a hundred, but eventually truth will again find expression, perhaps in a new word, or perhaps once more in an old word previously weakened by misuse and time.

For words are like wheat, and though a word may die, if it should return to the soil from which it came, it may find a new and glorious resurrection – and we may be reminded of truths all but forgotten.

The analogy is not perfect, but it has some merit, I think, by way of a preface to a brief consideration of the words of love in the New Testament, on our way to an enquiry into God's love for the world.

The New Testament was written in a unique season of world history, in which the Greek language was being blown by the strong cultural winds of the Roman Empire. It was now the lingua franca of the Empire and was being used – and misused – by many speakers of other native tongues. It is likely that the conventions

Concerning Words

of its use were fluid and varied throughout the Empire.

To complicate matters further, the writers of the New Testament were sailing in uncharted waters – as profound as they were original. They sought to communicate a new revelation of the mystery of God and His redemptive plan, and unlike the first great revelation, which was, by and large, on the national scale, theirs was a message that burst out on the scale of the world. To that end, they pressed into service the language with the most significant reach – the Koine Greek of the day.

Central to their theme was love, but not like any form of love the world had yet known. It was a love that came from the character of Godhead itself, and of a God unlike anything the Greeks had known – even when they were at their best, and those days were now distant.

It is true that the Romans had taken much of the Greek culture and made it their own, but it was weaker, less lofty and more mundane, and the language was changing in like manner. If the ground had been prepared for the expansion of Christianity by the universal adoption of the Greek language, that language had also lost much of its precision and nobility in the process.

It is against such a backdrop that the writers of the New Testament wrote, and it would be well for us to pause to ask whether there are any peculiarities that should be borne in mind, as we begin our enquiry.

The Purposeful Love of God

❧

When we consider how the writers of the New Testament used the Greek of their day, it quickly becomes apparent that it was indeed peculiar. As B.B. Warfield says, "...this body of literature stands out ... in a certain isolation. Neither in the secular literature of the early Christian centuries, nor even in the immediately succeeding religious literature ... is the change in usage anything like so manifest. We have an odd feeling that, with respect to the expression of the idea of love at least, the Greek of the New Testament ... has run ahead of its time, and ... seems more modern than that of even the Christian writers that came after them."*

That change is most conspicuously seen in the replacement of what might be called the *general term* for love. In the classical Greek language, there were several words for love, each of which conveyed love's essential nature, and in that sense, they were similes of each other. But each qualified love in a unique sense so that, although they could all be used in similar contexts, they each conveyed a particular character that could be brought into view when required.

However, in addition to this, one of these words was more predominant and was also used as a *general term*; when there was no particular need to qualify its character more finely. In classical Greek, this general

---

* B.B. Warfield, The Princeton Theological Review, v. xvi, 1918, p2

term was *philia*,* and as might be expected, it appears in the literature with a much higher frequency than the other similes.

The particular qualifying character of the general term, *philia*, tends towards the love of affection, as the love between brothers or good friends. It was not a love that was too lofty (*agape*) or too passionate (*eros*) so as to be uncomfortable or awkward in daily speech, and as such, it lent itself easily to use as a general term; being, relative to the other similes, somewhat middle of the road.

What all this means in practice is that the higher frequency of the word used as the general term for love tended to *de-emphasise* its own specific character, with the result that its unique character gradually receded into the background, though it perhaps never disappeared entirely from sight. Thus, if an author wished to emphasise the idea of brotherly love, extra effort was required to make it stand out – perhaps by bringing in one or more of the other similes by way of contrast, or by compounding as in the word, *philidelphia*, from *philia* (love) and *adelphos* (brother).

The point to take away is that one cannot automatically assume the more precise meaning in all occurrences of the word also used as a general term. In most cases, the word, *philia*, was simply to be understood

---

* For simplicity, I have used the noun forms of the Greek words throughout the book.

in its function as a universal concept or a place holder that was filled with meaning from the context itself, much like our own English word, love.

With this in mind, when we turn to the New Testament, we see something extremely interesting. "Without any heralding in the secular literature",* the roles have changed, and whereas *agape* was previously the simile least used of all the word group, in the New Testament we find that *agape* has supplanted the place of *philia* and has itself become the general term, while *philia* has become a lesser used simile.

Now, it would be easy to jump to the conclusion that this fact carries immense religious significance, but whatever significance this sudden change might have must be tempered by the fact that the Septuagint, translated from the Hebrew to early Koine Greek in the third century before Christ, exhibits the same pattern. Indeed, it broke the ground for its subsequent use in the New Testament. In other words, the adoption of *agape* as a general term had already become familiar to the New Testament writers, and they were simply continuing in the same habit and style.

Which raises the question, why did the translators of the Septuagint make such a departure from conventional Greek? Though the answers are probably many, common to them all will be a response to the culture of the day, and a desire, on the part of the Jewish translators, to

---

* B.B. Warfield, The Princeton Theological Review, v. xvi, 1918, p1

elevate their religious text above that culture.

※

There has been a suggestion that the use of *agape* had already become more dominant in the vernacular Greek before it appeared in the contemporary Greek literature. If this was the case, it is strange that the first written instances should appear in the translations of the holy scriptures of the Jewish people, who revered them as sacred. It is a notion that seems to run quite against the cultural biases of the Jewish people; who for thousands of years had ingrained in their psyche, the idea that they were a holy people, separate from the nations.

The Jews were not easily swayed by the cultures around them; indeed, there has always been a certain stubborn pride, not to say arrogance, resulting in a fierce resistance to assimilation. To even consider translating from the original Hebrew to Koine Greek would have been a difficulty not easily overcome, and doubtless, there would have been some religious leaders who never could support such an endeavour.

It is more reasonable to assume, in keeping with their national and religious psyche, that the Jews would be the ones conspicuously applying their own religious and cultural biases to the translation of their own holy scriptures, through the conscious and deliberate choice of whatever Greek words would best serve that purpose.

The Purposeful Love of God

And *agape*, with regard to its qualifying character, was the love that recognised value, or preciousness – as that of a precious metal – in the object loved[*], i.e., it more consistently pointed to the higher, more noble qualities in the idea of love. Hence, *agape*, used as the general term for love, tended towards the elevation of the concept of love in general and, as a result, separated and elevated the Greek translation from the common culture and Greek literature of the day – something that would have been self-recommending to devout Jewish scholars amid an increasingly brutish secular culture.

With these things in mind, it seems more natural to assume that the general use of *agape* in the Septuagint was, in large measure, something rather unique to the Jewish *religious* genre and that over the next few hundred years, Jewish religious culture became more familiar and comfortable with using *agape* as the general term for love, at least in the religious context; and that by the time the apostles wrote their own letters and gospels, it had become the normal style of expression they had grown accustomed to when writing in the religious genre.

---

[*] B.B. Warfield, The Princeton Theological Review, v. xvi, 1918

Concerning Words

If we follow this line of thought a little further, it might be expected that there would arise some degree of confusion concerning the use of *agape* among the Gentiles in the early churches, who were then converting to Christianity in large numbers – converts unfamiliar with the way *agape* was being used in the Jewish religious texts. And if this was the case, one might assume the new Jewish apostles and writers were aware of the issue, and would make some attempt at clarification or re-definition within their epistles, especially those written to non-Jewish readers.

Interestingly, there seems to be some evidence of this in the New Testament, especially in Paul's letters. In his first letter to the Corinthians, Paul writes, "If I speak with the tongues of mankind and of angels, but do not have love (*agape*), I have become a noisy gong or a clanging cymbal. If I have the gift of prophecy and know all mysteries and all knowledge, and if I have all faith so as to remove mountains, but do not have love (*agape*), I am nothing."*

And then, perhaps aware that the term, *agape*, was less familiar to his Gentile readers, Paul offered what can only be described as a comprehensive technical definition of the term: "Love (*agape*) is patient, love (*agape*) is kind, and is not jealous; love (*agape*) does not

---
*   1Cor. 13:1-3

The Purposeful Love of God

brag and is not arrogant, does not act unbecomingly; it does not seek its own, is not provoked, does not take into account a wrong suffered, does not rejoice in unrighteousness, but rejoices with the truth; bears all things, believes all things, hopes all things, endures all things. Love (*agape*) never fails".*

Now, over the centuries since this passage was first written it has taken on a significance that towers over much else in the New Testament. It has been called Paul's great Hymn of Love and is the subject of a sea of books and sermons that treat it with virtually mystical devotion. And while I will not go so far as to say that is wrong, I will say Paul was no mystic. He was not a theologian isolated from the practicalities of daily life. He was a scholar, yes, but the same hands that held the scrolls were hands calloused from the constant labour of tent-making and his concern for the churches was no less practical and mundane.

There are those who have taken this passage and redefined the word, *agape,* to equate it to God's unique love but, whatever else may be said, this passage does not define *agape* uniquely as God's love; rather, they are definitions applied in the very practical context of

---

* 1Cor. 13:4-8a

a believer's *experience*. Indeed, when Paul says love does not take into account a wrong suffered, he is manifestly not speaking of God's experience. For God *does* take account of wrongs suffered; if He did not, there would be no need for the cross.

John also, in his own inimitable style, has a habit of defining *agape* in very practical ways. He writes, "God is love (*agape*)", and then immediately defines the word, "In this is love (*agape*), ... that He loved us and sent His Son to be the propitiation for our sins." *

And when John says God is love, he is not equating God and love. Love, even *agape* love, is not God. John is instead, defining the quality of God's love as being of the very highest – which means, for John, *agape* love. He goes on to explain that, from the point of view of *God's* experience, it was a love characterised by the action of holiness in sending His Son to be the propitiation for our sins.

For John is aware of the limitations of the words he is using and, to his mind, even *agape* is not sufficient to convey the truth he intends; he is compelled to add a clarifying explanation, made necessary by the use of *agape* as the general term for love, and from an awareness that many outside the Jewish religious tradition would find it unfamiliar.

Again, John, like Paul, also speaks of *agape* from the practical point of view of *our* experience: "For this is the

---

* 1Jn 4:8b,10

love (*agape*) of God, that we keep His commandments".*
Again, "love (*agape*) one another. And this is love (*agape*), that we walk according to His commandments".†

In the above passages, John is careful to clarify what he means by his use of *agape*. He explains it as an effectual love, the kind of love that results in actions that are in harmony with God's law.

What I have written above is not meant to be exhaustive. It is offered here by way of an introduction, to provide a brief background to the words we have come to take for granted, and to give a sense of history to help make us aware that words – even biblical words – are not without limitation.

What, then, can be said concerning the language used in early Christian writing? Firstly, that none of the examples above represent *theological* definitions, rather, they may simply represent a practical effort to clarify the meaning of *agape*, taken as a general term. Therefore, we need to be cautious before attributing any narrow theological significance to the word, *agape*, in the New Testament.

Secondly, with respect to the word, *agape*, it is likely

---

* 1Jn 5:3a
† 2Jn 1:5b,6

Concerning Words

that any special character it once held may have faded and should no longer automatically be assumed in most instances. However, this may be over-stating things somewhat because it is evident that the writers of the New Testament had a very high regard for this term for love, and it had, over several hundred years, come to hold a special place in Jewish religious thought, that was relatively unknown in the general culture of the day, but had once again begun to develop a new life of its own.

Further, it is evident that the writers of the New Testament made deliberate efforts, likely for those unfamiliar with its Jewish religious usage, to define or redefine that general term as the love of the highest and most noble quality. Further still, this high quality was now attached to the term in general, so that the general concept of love in the New Testament is everywhere elevated, both with regard to humanity as well as God.

But apart from this general elevation and ennobling of the concept of love, we can say little more specifically with regard to the *character* of God's love, except to say that God's love is *holy*, and of the very highest quality – something we might have inferred without any knowledge of Greek whatsoever.

And perhaps it is fitting that it should be so, for otherwise, truth might rest disproportionately in the hands of the scholars, and for all the debt the Christian church owes to scholarship, they are not the sole mediators of truth. God offers Himself to the whole world – to the intellectual and the simple-minded alike – and words alone are too limited for that.

If we are to go any deeper, it is to pictures we must turn our attention – or, more precisely, to the use of metaphor.

Now, a metaphor describes attributes and character by the use of comparison to a shared experience. It *assumes* a common experience, or at least an appreciation of it, and if that appreciation is shared by the race in general, to the same extent, the metaphor is capable of revealing truth. Rich or poor, clever or not, it matters little – all who can share or appreciate the experience can perceive the truth in a metaphor.

But here again, we find scripture has not left the idea of metaphor unchanged by religious thought. While the Bible often uses a metaphor in the common literary sense, it also employs the device in a more profound and unique way.

The writers of the New Testament speak of *copies* or *shadows* in our world – shadows of something real in the heavenly realm. The apostle Paul can speak of, "food or drink or in respect to a festival or a new moon or a Sabbath day – things which are a *mere* shadow of what

CONCERNING WORDS

is to come; but the substance belongs to Christ."*

Therefore, when the Bible speaks metaphorically, for instance, of God the Father, we need to be aware that the concept of fatherhood originates in heaven, and what we know as fatherhood on earth is merely a shadow of the actual reality. God is "*the* Father, from whom every family in heaven and on earth derives its name." †

What this means for us is twofold. Firstly, it again elevates biblical language beyond the familiar metaphor, making the comparison more poignant and powerful as we realise these shadows have been deliberately placed within our world as a means of revelation – pointing to something actual and real in the heavenly realm.

Secondly, the fact that they are 'mere' shadows means they are necessarily also limited in the scope of the revelation that is possible. That is to say, our own personal experience, or even the collective experience of the race, cannot be the final arbiter of truth.

There will inevitably be aspects of our human experience that do not reflect the heavenly reality. Therefore, even in the metaphors used in scripture, there is a sense in which they can be said to be used as a general term. And while there may be significant overlap of the concepts the writers are attempting to convey, we should not be surprised if there are also differences that require further clarification, perhaps provided by the

---

* Col 2:16-17 (Emphasis added)
† Eph. 3:14–15 (Emphasis added)

New Testament authors themselves.

It is with caution then, that we proceed to the metaphorical, paying particular attention to any modifications and clarifications that scripture places upon them.

CHAPTER II

The Husband

N ANCIENT SOCIETIES the marriage covenant was a binding contract, though not necessarily permanent. Its terms were commonly negotiated between the heads of families, often in fine detail, which included provisions for financial arrangements and respective ownership rights – both for the bride and groom – in the event the covenant was broken or terminated. These were, typically, arranged marriages, but for the most part, they were not forced marriages; the bride's wishes were usually taken into account.

We see this, for example, in the biblical record when Abraham's servant journeys to find a wife for his master's son, Isaac. Though the negotiations are between the servant (as Abraham's proxy) and Bethuel and Laban (Rebekah's father and brother, respectively), Rebekah is nonetheless consulted to determine her wishes, and she has the final say. However, once the commitment had been made and all terms agreed to, and after the marriage was consummated, it was a contract legally binding on both parties.

Today in the West, there is a tendency to think the prenuptial agreement slightly distasteful, that there is something not quite right about it, and anyway, in the modern world, we marry for love, and we are therefore so much better than the ancients.

This is merely the illusion of an unreflective modern mind. The reason a prenuptial agreement is redundant for most marriages in the West today is not that we are any better or because we marry for love, but because today in the West, both parties' rights and obligations have been enshrined in common law. Instead of families negotiating the terms of the marriage contract between themselves with the bride and groom, we have now standardised the agreement in the law of the land. All that is now necessary to enter into that standardised legal contract is to sign a registry and receive a certificate.

That is really what that 'piece of paper' is all about. Indeed, when couples in the West began eschewing the marriage certificate for the 'de facto' marriage, it did not take long for many of them to realise the importance of those legal protections and soon begin to petition governments for legal recognition – sans certificate.

So, one way or another, marriage has always been, and always will be, a covenant that binds the husband and wife with certain rights and obligations. That fact may be lost on many young couples today, because time and habit have removed it from the modern consciousness, but for the ancients, these things were still very much in the fabric of their everyday lives.

It is not surprising, then, that when we first see marriage used as a metaphor in the Bible, it is in relation to the idea of covenant.

It was first introduced through the prophet Hosea in the Old Testament, who used it to illustrate something of the relationship between God and His people, within the context of Israel's unfaithfulness to the covenant at Sinai.

On its face, it might seem reasonable that the metaphor would suggest itself easily to the prophet's mind. Still, when one considers the pagan religions, in which the gods were just as likely to behave as corruptly and immorally as humanity, it is probable that the prophet opposed the association and had legitimate grounds to reject the metaphor altogether. After all, the God of Israel was far removed in kind from the heathen gods, and to suggest the metaphor was to open up all manner of unholy associations between God and His people – something Hosea is likely to have found abhorrent.

This may explain, in part, the extraordinary lengths

The Purposeful Love of God

to which God went to bring the metaphor to Hosea's mind because Hosea did not, by his own volition, apply the metaphor to the covenant relationship of God and Israel; the metaphor was pressed upon him by the express command of God, not in a prosaic way, but with all the full, painful force of cruel experience.

For God's purpose, it was not enough that Hosea simply delivered an objective message to the people of Israel. It was imperative that the people felt the guilt of their crime. God did not wish them to simply understand the message, He wanted it to cut them to the quick. They must needs feel His anger, His grief, His love betrayed, and in such a way that all but the hardest of hearts would empathise with Him and take His side. And the metaphor of the marriage relationship is more suited to those ends than any other – it was already written into the history and experience of mankind, both the promise and the pain.

But a story observed through time becomes dull. The people needed to see it lived out among them – in all its sordid detail. And that would be the task of the hapless prophet. Therefore, it was essential for Hosea to first live it and be overwhelmed by it. He must share in the same experience, or something as close to it as could be contrived.

The metaphor would not be left as a vague generality, but would be narrowed to one specific and very real case. It was not a suggestion, it was not optional, and it

The Husband

was not temporary. Hosea was to live it out over many years – it would become his life. And the unfairness of the task would only add to the force of the message he would eventually proclaim. And so, to create that very specific metaphor, God commanded Hosea to marry a harlot. And the prophet obeyed.

It is interesting that God did not name her, but left the choice to Hosea himself; he chose a woman by the name of Gomer. We can only speculate whether there was already some history between them, but it is not unlikely. Perhaps, they had known each other from her youth and had been friends until their paths diverged as the circumstances and choices of life conspired to drive a wedge between them, and she found herself on a path that Hosea could not travel, but could only observe from a distance, and with pity. Whatever the history between them, it is at least clear from the very beginning that Hosea already loved her, and as the years passed, Hosea's love for Gomer would continue to grow.

However, though Gomer was willing to enter into the covenant relationship and marry Hosea, it is equally clear that Gomer did not value or return that love. She eventually betrayed him and despised it altogether, abandoning Hosea to return to a life of prostitution. But it did not go well for Gomer; her former lovers did not receive her as they once had. She was shunned and mistreated until she was left with nothing. Alone and destitute, she was eventually reduced to the life of a slave.

How long she lived this way is unknown, but if God was determined to drive home the lesson (and He was), it may have been significant. All the while, Hosea's love was undiminished, though he did not intervene, not until Gomer had been brought to a place that made her redemption possible. And when at last that time had come, God spoke to Hosea again, saying, "Go again, love a woman who is loved by her husband, yet an adulteress, even as the LORD loves the sons of Israel, though they turn to other gods".[*]

So, the prophet found her, and paying the price demanded, bought her for himself and brought her home.

This is the back plot to the book of Hosea, and his personal story is told in the first few chapters before the prophet goes on to speak more directly to the nation. God deemed it necessary for His own purposes. As a result, Hosea's message to the people of Israel was infused with a passion, a tenderness, and a power and severity, that is hard to ignore or overstate. And we who read his words today are invited to see God's love for His

---

[*] Hos 3:1

The Husband

people through this very specific metaphor of marriage.

It is not just any marriage, certainly not the marriage that we would choose – not the metaphor of the ideal or perfect marriage; that would be too neat to be real. But it is to this particular marriage that we are introduced, in order to see God's side of the story. There is nothing soft or flattering in its portrayal, nothing to make us feel good about ourselves. Yes, there is redemption, even forgiveness, but nothing is glossed over, and nothing forgotten. It is the story of the history of God's people, written for our warning but also our hope, and it is within this extraordinary example that we begin to see the character of God's love in a way that would not be possible otherwise.

In the Septuagint, the word used in the text for this love is the Greek word, *agape* – the word used in classical times of the love born out of a recognition of the worth of the object loved. But there is something in this story that makes the word choice ironic, even euphemistic. Surely, there is nothing of that kind of love to be suggested by such a story as this. Indeed, there is nothing in Gomer worthy to be loved; no gold that makes that love comprehensible, no worth that makes it justifiable. No, in this context, *agape* has none of its former meaning. The word is used here because it is

The Purposeful Love of God

employed simply as a general term for love, a placeholder – leaving the content of its meaning to be drawn out from the context and metaphor of the story.

And that meaning is striking. "Go again, love a woman *who is loved by her husband*".* Hosea *loved* Gomer, though there was nothing she had done to deserve his love, and everything she had done to extinguish it. Yet, he continued to love her, nevertheless.

In classical times, the word that would have undoubtedly been used to describe such a love was the Greek word, *eros*. It was a word that qualified love in terms of passion or devotion. Naturally, it could be used for the sensual love between a man and woman, and in time, it came to be so used almost exclusively, at least within the popular culture – which is why we do not find it in the Septuagint translation. But it was not historically a base word or reserved only for such use, any more than the other Greek similes for love. In earlier times, it could also be used for a passionate love of the highest quality and purity, a love both noble and worthy, "that high love of exalted devotion which, from this point of view, soars above all other love."†

It is a love, not justified by reason of the worth of the object loved, but existing in and of itself. It is not created by any outside agency or influence but is willed spontaneously and joyfully of itself, without effort or

---

* Hos 3:1 (Emphasis added)
† B.B. Warfield, The Princeton Theological Review, v. xvi, 1918

self-reflection. As such, it is a love that is greater and reaches higher even than *agape*. This is the kind of love we have represented in the story of Hosea and Gomer.

But there is something in the metaphor that points us beyond even this kind of exalted love, something in the story's tragedy that magnifies it further still. I do not speak of the tragedy of Gomer – the tragedy of a wife who shows no appreciation, gratitude, or even awareness of the grace extended to her, and finally, who shows only contempt and betrayal of that love. That is tragic enough, but it is at least understandable. The greater tragedy, and that which is felt more keenly, lies not in the pride and wretchedness of Gomer but in the undying love of her husband, whose love, through all the shame, jealousy and betrayal, is not in the least diminished but rather shows itself to be utterly boundless and unquenchable.

That is tragedy Shakespeare could have been proud of, but it can leave us with more pity for Hosea than for Gomer, which, of course, is precisely the intent; it invites us to take God's side. But not through pity alone. Left to pity, our easy conclusion is to assume he was somehow blind to her crimes – blinded by the passion of his love – but there is something here, a principle perhaps, that lies beneath the surface and underscores the long, unhappy tale.

There is no note of the naïve here, which would help us understand and excuse Hosea's love. He is not in the least blind or numb to her betrayal, and for all his passion, he remains on the side of righteousness – and in the end, that means judgment. Indeed, the fact that he does not turn his eyes away from the magnitude of her sin, and from judgment, makes his love all the more difficult to comprehend. Yes, his love is passionate, it is *eros* in the pure sense, but it is not *devotion*. His passion is not the ruling principle. He is not ruled by the weakness of obsession or even pity – and he is not ruled by sentiment.

Those are things that would make his love more understandable, but again, they are entirely absent from the narrative. We see here, instead, a power, even a purpose, in his love that hints at some greater principle, a principle that is itself the genesis of that passion, a principle that rules over it and subsumes it to itself.

For when, in the course of the story, the covenant is broken, there is no hint of a wish to set aside justice or judgment, though his love does not waver or diminish. Again, it is not the love of sentiment or devotion, and therefore a weaker kind of love, prone to blindness and too willing to bend. Indeed, it is a love that does not simply endure through judgment but *abides* in it.

The Husband

It is difficult to speak of such a love because it seems strange to us that love should embrace law – that love should *require* it. I suppose it has been written somewhere about God that law and love are two sides of the same coin, as if we only see one or the other at any one moment in time. But that is not the sense conveyed here.

Here, there is no sense of the two being opposites – one manifest to the exclusion of the other – rather, they are set before us as existing one within, and in complete agreement with, the other. There is a greater principle and purpose they both emanate from, and wholly serve. There is no conflict between them, no tension, only an extraordinary agreement and harmony. It is justice with the blessing of mercy. It is, in the classical sense, *eros* with the blessing of the holy.

That makes His love something so much more worthy of our respect than our pity. And it puts it in a new category as it strains the limits of the metaphor. It is set before us – choreographed for our instruction through the life of a prophet – so that we might have a glimpse of what we so mundanely call the love of God.

But it is only a glimpse, a beginning, if you will. Hosea's story does not tell the whole; we are deliberately left without any true resolution but instead, with the uneasy feeling of an uncertain future. At best, at the end of the prophet's tale, there has been only a partial restoration. Gomer is freed from the bondage of her past, but she has not been fully restored to her former status as Hosea's wife. For that to happen, something else will be required. We are not told what that is – a decision perhaps, or maybe a sincere change of heart – but whatever it is, it appears she is now on probation for many days to come.

This probationary period was not the end of Gomer's personal story, but for God's purposes, it was the climax of the message He wanted Israel to understand and feel. Israel was being offered one last chance to prove to God that His love was not wasted upon them. God was now waiting to see how they would respond to that message.

If they responded well, they would be reinstated to their original place as a true wife, a partner with God in His great work, and not simply a servant. But it was by no means a certainty, and left with that uncertainty, the story hints at something beyond our own interests, something beyond our own need, something that speaks more to God's interest, and what He is prepared to do to accomplish that end.

CHAPTER III

THE FATHER

ATHER IS USED as a metaphor for God perhaps a dozen times in the Old Testament. It is enough to make the idea known but not enough to make it common, and one gets the sense from the New Testament that the Jewish leaders, while generally accepting its use, were not entirely comfortable with its *everyday* use, which is how it began to be used by Jesus and His disciples.

But if that was all there was to it, they might have eventually come to make peace with its increasingly frequent, and casual use. What they could not abide, was the blasphemous way Jesus appropriated the title 'Father' to describe, without any hint of the metaphoric, His relation to God, making Himself out to be the unique Son of God. This incensed the Jewish leaders, for they understood what it meant – it was tantamount to making Himself equal to God.

Yet, all who came to follow Jesus recognised Him as

the only begotten Son from the Father.* They somehow saw the truth despite its incomprehensibility. And to all who received Him as the unique Son of God, Jesus elevated them to brethren, effectively adopting them into His family circle with the Father in heaven. He taught them to pray, "Our Father who is in heaven",† and from that time forward, the use of 'Father' has become one of the distinguishing features of the Christian religion. Through the centuries, it has become so habitual and natural in the language of the church that it has become God's proper title, and its role as a metaphor is seldom emphasised or distinguished.

Yet, the distinction does remain, partly because our direct experience is only that of our own earthly fathers, and whatever else God may be, He is undoubtedly more than even the best of these. Partly too, because there is still a vague awareness of the presumption, not to say chutzpah, of calling the holy God of heaven our Father, and also, because there is a careful attitude of respect surrounding the term written into the New Testament by the authors themselves.

They use the word freely but not in isolation from the broader, absolute context. For example, it is frequently used in close proximity with the generic term for deity, as if we need to hold them both in our minds simultaneously. The connection is especially close with

---

* See Jn 1:14
† Matt 6:9

The Father

Paul: "Grace to you and peace from God our Father".*
There is a habit in their writing that reminds us that the term, 'Father', is a privileged title, best grounded in reality: "Yet for us there is but one God, the Father, from whom are all things and we exist for Him".†

※

However, there is no question that 'Father' is the most natural of the metaphors used to describe our relation to God. Certainly, it is more natural than the metaphor of the husband – and by more natural, I mean it sits closer in our minds to the reality it seeks to convey. For instance, we trace our existence to our own earthly fathers; that is, there is a *creative* aspect to the relationship.

There is also a more natural parallel in the hierarchy of authority. We are born into that authority by virtue of our dependency, and at least in our childhood, authority is vested in our earthly fathers – and that, without our consent.

Contrast this with the metaphor of the husband of the previous chapter, where authority – even if it is still weighted toward the husband – is at least entered into by the consent of both parties, and because of which, might

---
* Phil 1:2
† 1 Cor 8:6

perhaps be described as a kind of shared authority. But that is not the idea in fatherhood, which, as a metaphor, has better and closer parallels to the absolute hierarchy that necessarily exists between God and His creation.

But fatherhood, as a metaphor, informs that hierarchy and softens it. The authority of a father is the authority of governorship rather than the authority of lordship – we are born into a father's management and care, which means into his love, more so than into his service. Indeed, wherever the term is employed in the Bible, the implication is always of a loving, benevolent Father. That is one of the insights from the elder brother in Jesus' parable of the prodigal son.

But the metaphor is also more natural for another reason: it is closer to nature itself. Fatherhood has been written into nature – and into *our* nature – at the most fundamental level. We must be taught many things, but the idea of fatherhood is not one of them, even for a fallen humanity. Jesus says as much when He says, "If you then, being evil, know how to give good gifts to your children, how much more will your Father who is in heaven give what is good to those who ask Him!"*

It is that love within nature that ties family

---

* Matt 7:11

together. The Greeks thought it worthy enough to give it its own word, *storge*; the love that encompasses all the loyalties and obligations that come with those ties. It is capable of great tenderness and affection but also, when necessary, a fierce and selfless protection for those under its care. And because it is natural, it also extends to that instinctual love that can be found in the animal kingdom in general – as, for instance, that kind of love which exists between the lioness and her cubs. To put it paradoxically, it is that obligatory love that nonetheless arises naturally and is offered freely.

So the question becomes, how far can this idea be applied, by metaphor, to our Father in heaven?

❧

When the church uses the metaphor in her language today, it is used with a sense of the inevitability of God's love toward us, and for all mankind. But is His love really eternally directed toward His children, whatever our guilt or shame, because, like us, it is simply in His nature to love His children, whatever they do?

It may seem that the answer is obvious and should be given in the affirmative, but if that is the case, it is curious that not one of the authors of the New Testament should use the word, *storge*, not even once, in connection with the love of the Father for His own.

To explore this question further, I turn the reader's

attention to the parable of the prodigal son. It is one of the most widely known of all of Jesus' parables and holds a special place in the hearts of believers, and even non-believers, for its comforting message of God's willingness to forgive. It is one of the few instances of Jesus' teaching that offends no one – which is probably reason enough to suspect that we may be missing something. Nonetheless, it is where many Christians find one of the most full and unrestrained displays of God's love, even in the face of the ruin and contempt of His sons.

Thus, it stands to reason that this parable can shed light on the answers to the question above, but there are also other reasons to look at it. Firstly, whatever else it reveals to us of the Father's love, it also shows us how Jesus Himself uses the metaphor, and therefore serves as an exemplar for us – and if, perchance, there should be any limitation upon its use, that limitation would come with the express authority of Jesus' own words.

However, before we look at the parable directly, we had best look at the context in which it was set. When we do, it is the first point of interest to note that the parable is not directly concerned with love or forgiveness, but its concern is with the attitude of the righteous toward a sinner who repents. Jesus told the parable in response to the grumblings of the indignant religious leaders; that sinners should, so quickly and freely, be brought back into the company of the righteous.

A second point of interest is that this parable was told as the last of a group of three. Therefore, a brief look at the preceding parables in the group will help us by way of comparison.

※

In the first of three parables,* Jesus describes a shepherd who leaves his flock to find one lost sheep out of a hundred. When he finds it, he brings it back home on his shoulders. He then gathers together his friends and neighbours saying, "Rejoice with me, because I have found my sheep which was lost!" After which, Jesus formally states the point of the parable: "I tell you that in the same way, there will be more joy in heaven over one sinner who repents than over ninety-nine righteous persons who need no repentance." The message is clear: the Scribes and Pharasees should rejoice that repentant sinners have been restored to the company of the righteous.

Jesus follows immediately with the parable of a woman who lost a silver coin and swept her whole house searching for it until it was found. After which, she also gathers her friends and neighbours, saying, "Rejoice with me, for I have found the coin which I had lost!" And Jesus once again restates the point He was

---

* See Luke 15

making, saying, "In the same way, I tell you, there is joy in the presence of the angels of God over one sinner who repents."

It is only after Jesus has made His point clear that He tells the extended and more detailed parable of the prodigal son, which, because of the preceding two parables, did not require its central point to be formally reiterated at its conclusion. Instead, Jesus restates it from within the story itself: "Son, you have always been with me, and all that is mine is yours. But we had to celebrate and rejoice, for this brother of yours was dead and has begun to live, and was lost and has been found."

Thus, in all three parables, Jesus is directing his message to the religious rulers, saying they should not grumble but rejoice when a sinner repents. It is plain, then, that the parable of the prodigal son does not stand on its own, and if we are to look for any particular quality of God's love within it, we should do so with one eye also on the preceding parables. For if Jesus considered it necessary to present His ideas through these three parables together, we may reasonably conclude that He thought each, in some way, insufficient on its own.

If there is some insufficiency, it is not in the clarity of the meaning behind the parables. That meaning is clear from the first and second, where Jesus explicitly declared – somewhat uncharacteristically – the main teaching point at the conclusion of each.

The three-fold emphasis is likely due to the fact that, taken in isolation, each parable only partially represented the character of the Father He knew by experience. And perhaps for our benefit, but more likely to be true to His own experience, Jesus employed these three parables because, while insufficient in themselves, they were more to His own satisfaction when taken together.

For though love is not the central theme of the parables, the character of God's love can be seen through the *pity* of a shepherd for his sheep, and in the *value* placed upon the silver coin, and again, it can be seen through the *love* of a father for his son. But neither one of these – really, not even all of them taken together – are sufficient to tell the whole of God's love. They are, after all, only metaphors, even if one of them is so familiar to our experience.

And it is precisely because we are so familiar with the idea of fatherhood that we should approach it with care, lest we inadvertently gloss over any insufficiency or clarification in the metaphor with our familiar but overconfident sentiment. For it is easy to warm towards the figure of a loving, benevolent father and assume God's love is simply an infinite multiple of the same, without any qualification. In contrast, however, I do not think anyone would suggest we should think of God as a woman worried about the loss of her savings.

What then of the idea that the metaphors might be insufficient in some way when we come to apply them to God? It is not hard to find in the parable of the woman, and therefore there is little danger of stretching it further than its usefulness requires. Likewise, the parable of the shepherd and his sheep is also seen for nothing more than the metaphor that it is – we understand that we are more to God than witless sheep, and He is more than a shepherd whose entire duty is consumed by the care of such creatures. But it is not so easy to see how a father's love for his son could be in any way insufficient to describe the character of our heavenly Father, that character which Jesus knew through His own abiding experience.

And yet, taken together with the first two parables, something a little odd stands out in the telling of the parable of the prodigal son. That 'something' is the detail in the narrative of how the prodigal son is found, compared to the finding of the object in the first two parables. Something very unexpected, yet deliberate on Jesus' part, and therefore extremely significant, that runs quite against our natural idea of a father's love, and thus, has far-reaching implications as to how we understand the love of God, and by extension, God Himself.

The Father

We know that in all three, there is something lost that is found. A shepherd has lost a sheep and actively searches until he finds it, returning it to the flock upon his shoulders. Again, a woman has lost a silver coin and actively searches for it until she finds it.

The finding and returning in both cases were solely the result of the action of the shepherd and woman, respectively – the sheep and the coin are passive and have no part in their own recovery. In fact, it is not hard to imagine the sheep was brought back even against its own will.

However, there is a change in the narrative regarding the finding of the prodigal son. For, as Jesus tells it, the father does *not* actively seek for the son. If the son was lost and then found, it can be more accurately said that the son found himself, and of his own volition, began his journey home. Only after the son had already made the greater part of the journey from a "distant country" did the father see him from afar and make haste to go to him and welcome him home with joy and celebration.

Now, it might be said that there is nothing oddly significant in this parable because it is evident that a coin cannot find itself, and of course, a witless sheep must necessarily be actively sought for and brought back into the fold. In those cases, we can expect the narrative to run along no other lines. But what is curious, and if we are honest, not a little disconcerting, is why Jesus did not simply continue with the same narrative as the shepherd and the woman, and portray the father actively searching for his son, in a similar way to the sheep. It would have made no difference to the parable's meaning – which we have already seen was unrelated to the method of recovery, but to the joy of its accomplishment.

Concerning the love of the father, it would only have magnified the father's love all the more if Jesus portrayed the father actively searching for his lost son. But Jesus' construction of the parable shows the father initially in an unsympathetic light, almost indifferent to the son's self-made ruin – all of which tends toward something deficient, something wanting, in a father's natural love, and not toward its magnification. For what loving father would not hasten to search for his lost and ruined son to bring him back to the safety and shelter of his family home?

This change in narrative becomes all the more conspicuous when one considers Jesus' mastery of the Hebrew scriptures. Undoubtedly, even in the very formation and telling of the parable, Jesus' mind must have recalled the story set before us in the previous chapter. For the story of Hosea and his wife, Gomer, has such similarities in its structure that it could have been the very inspiration for Jesus' new parable on this great theme of redemption.

Gomer, like the prodigal son, also forsook her privileged position and ran away to a life of loose living. Likewise, she eventually lost everything and became destitute. Perhaps, most interestingly, both came, in the end, to be servants of the ones they had previously despised, and who had been their access and right to their former position – literally for Gomer and at least in attitude for the prodigal son. Both were once lost and then found.

Indeed, the narratives are so similar that it is hard to believe Jesus was not drawing on Gomer's story for His own construction of the parable of the prodigal son. And, of course, Jesus was familiar with the mode of Gomer's return; how she was actively and deliberately sought for and found by Hosea, who ransomed her and brought her back home.

That is the familiar gospel that so comforts and enthrals the church. It is also in line with the parable of the lost sheep. Surely, it would have been the most natural and straightforward course to continue along the same lines; telling the story of a loving father who searched for his lost son, ransomed him, and brought him home. Yet, surprisingly, disconcertingly, Jesus inserted, as if from nowhere, a new narrative that presents, at least on the face of it, the picture of a somewhat different – not to say colder – father.

The Purposeful Love of God

❧

Perhaps, if we had only read the parable in isolation, it would be easy to pass over the significance of what Jesus is saying but taken together with the first two parables, and again with the story of Gomer's restoration, the departure in the narrative constructed for the return of the prodigal son now becomes conspicuous to the point of requiring explanation.

And it is here that we begin to see the possibility of an insufficiency in the metaphor of the father, and further, an insufficiency that is not insignificant but strikes at the very heart of what defines a father's natural love; that love the Greeks knew as *storge*, and which, though well-suited and necessary within its context of nurture and governorship, we now begin to see, through the mind of Christ, is not wholly applicable when transferred to the grand theme of redemption.

For Jesus, deliberately and with unexpected force, departs from what is commonly expected of a father's love; a love that often does, far too easily by the sheer force of that love, pass over the demands of righteousness, as if love covers all. Its strength is its weakness – it is not strong enough, in a moral sense. And Jesus declares through this parable that what is all too common for an earthly father to do for his child, our heavenly Father will *not* do.

Just how intractable and unyielding His position

is, can be seen in Jesus' description of the son's relation to the father while the son is still in his sin. Jesus tells us the son was not simply lost but *dead* to the father and, by extension, to his love. In that pronouncement, there is a terrible but deliberate act of the father's will, a conscious and awful decision on the father's part to consider the son dead, and therefore, outside the father's love. Jesus pushes the narrative to an extreme – which, again, is otherwise unnecessary to the central theme of the parable, and by so doing, He makes the separation from the father's love not merely relative but *absolute*.

If that cuts deep into our modern sentiment, it probably also did for those who were there that day, listening to His words. It would not have been something easy to mistake or forget. John, the apostle who gave us "God is love",* seems to recall the force of Jesus' parable when he writes, "Do not love the world nor the things in the world. If anyone loves the world, the love of the Father is not in him."†

Yes, God's love is seen in this parable through the metaphor of the father, in the joy over the return of his prodigal son, and in the freeness of the father's forgiveness upon the son's return – first to his senses, and then to his home. But Jesus, with deliberate and remarkable bluntness, went out of His way to qualify the metaphor through a most unexpected modification

---

* 1 Jn 4:8
† 1 Jn 2:15

that cuts like a knife through our cherished ideals of fatherhood. But if Jesus knew it would be a shock to our sensibilities, that was not the reason for its telling.

It was fashioned more for Jesus' own sake, flowing naturally out of His own personal experience of His Father in heaven. The character of the father in the parable was in no sense contrived for dramatic effect, but spontaneously took on the moral character of the Father Jesus knew so well by experience; that is, "*the* Father, from whom every family in heaven and on earth derives its name".* That is to say, Jesus shaped the parable in such a way that reflected *His* reality and therefore, the true reality of Fatherhood itself.

It is a picture of fatherhood that is in many ways far removed from our own ideal, for the picture Jesus sets forth is of a *Holy* Father, who, though He is ready to forgive and willing that all should abide in His love, nevertheless places certain *conditions* upon it.

What those conditions might be are also laid out for us: they are simply the beauty of a contrite heart and the repentance it produces. But the father would make no direct intervention to force it from his son. The son must come to it by his own volition. It was the condition upon which his return to the father depended, and the son knew it to be so.

---

* Eph 3:14b–15 (emphasis added)

The Father

It is at this point that the parable sheds light upon the previously unresolved story of Gomer, whom the reader will remember was found and brought back by Hosea, but brought back only to remain as a servant on probation, with her future both uncertain and precarious. Or, to put it in the context of the prophecy to Israel, God was waiting to see if they also would repent with genuine humility and contrition.

In the parable of the prodigal son, the son met that condition and was restored to his father with great joy and celebration. This is what we expect from a loving father – it is not surprising. However, what is surprising is that Jesus made the father's love contingent upon the attitude and the repentance of the son; it was only after repentance that the son had "begun to live" to the father and was, therefore, once more able to abide in the father's love.

All of this points to the Holy Father's *moral* love; a love that is governed by His holy will as love's foundation. Again, this does not sit well with our modern sentiment, but it does highlight something we have already seen. I have noted the close connection between the parable and the story of Gomer. Both reveal the love of God in different ways, each with specific details within their own context. However, as to the self-limiting of His love, both have a remarkable consistency underlying

The Purposeful Love of God

them both.

In each, we see God's love, abundant and overflowing with the possibility of forgiveness and future blessing, but both are also contingent upon certain conditions imposed by God Himself. I repeat, imposed *by* God, not on God, as if there is some objective demand of righteousness outside His own will. But that would be nonsense, because there is nothing – no demand, no higher or objective principle, not even from within Himself – that constrains His will against the pleading of His love. There is no such conflict within God. God loves *because* He is holy.

Thus, the metaphor of the father communicates something real and meaningful about the character of God's love. God *is* our Father, and like an earthly father, He is kindly disposed towards us with a genuine concern for our well-being. But if there is any weakness in the metaphor, it is that it goes too far; it overlays too human a sentiment over the holiness of God.

The Fatherhood of God has a character beyond the reach of our own natural ideal of fatherhood – not merely in degree but also in kind; something that Jesus made evident through His effort to qualify the metaphor in the telling of the parable. And that is the point. Whatever our ideals of fatherhood, and the love associated with it, those ideals can only take us so far before we are faced with the holy *character* of God.

When it comes to redemption, at least on the world scale, our ideal of a father's natural love is insufficient to our great and dreadful need, and more to the point, insufficient to God's. Faced with the magnitude of sin on the scale of the race, it breaks down and fails, not because He is unwilling but because it is not the full measure of the holy character of God. Our natural ideal of fatherhood and a father's love (*storge*) is inadequate to that task. And it is Jesus, in the telling of the parable of the prodigal son, who brings this to our attention. It is why this kind of love (*storge*) does not appear in the New Testament.

Therefore, wherever the metaphor of the father is used, it should always be understood in the light of the modification that Jesus Himself placed upon it. What is more, through Jesus' own words, we come to the terrible understanding that there is nothing inevitable about our Father's love, but that His love rests upon the foundation of His own holy will – which is to say, He *chooses* to love, and therefore, He can also choose not to love.

By this, we understand His love is not the sum character of God, any more than love is the sum character of any man. His love is just that, *His*, and He makes it what it is by His own unique and holy character, and not the other way around. For God is more even than love, and it is through His own will, and for His own purposes, that love serves Him according to *His* character – and serves Him with a whole heart, no less than His righteousness.

CHAPTER IV

THE ARTISAN

PART I

"The heavens are telling of the glory of God;
And their expanse is declaring the work of His hands."

(Ps 19:1)

"Then God saw all that He had made, and behold, it was very good."

(Gen 1:31)

O SPEAK OF God as Creator is to express our relation to Him in its most fundamental form. It carries the idea of hierarchy more than creativity per se, and whatever it reveals about His creativity, it is creativity in an absolute sense; that is, He has created, out of nothing, everything. Which places Him in a unique, and primary place. He alone is the

Creator, and all else fills the lesser place of the created.

We also observe, through the created universe, His awesome power, and the exquisite yet unapproachable beauty of all creation, but these things can often leave us with an overwhelming sense of the vast separation between us, and of our utter smallness and insignificance. Of course, that is a response that is entirely justified; it would be obscene arrogance that did not feel that way when confronted by the raw power and wonder of creation. But it offers little insight into the *character* of the Being behind creation. The created universe witnesses chiefly to His existence and glory, not to His character. Creation provides no means of connection and no common ground. On the contrary, it can often do more to obscure His character.

But to see Him through the metaphor of the artisan, presents an opportunity to glimpse something of His creative *character*. It is true that the Bible does not use the word 'artisan' to describe God, but though it does not speak explicitly of God by that term, it does, everywhere, imply it. It uses words such as: Maker, Creator, Architect, Builder, and even Potter. And what are these, taken together, except the description of the greatest of all artisans?

It was His Spirit – the Spirit of the artisan – which was put into the Hebrew artisans in the desert that enabled the fashioning of the great works of the tabernacle. So, to speak of God as an artisan is merely

The Artisan

to consolidate, into one name, all the various ways scripture calls our attention to His creativity. God is *the* Artisan – to borrow from Paul – from whom all artisans in heaven and earth are named.

But what, exactly, is an artisan? The carpenter and the potter may have skill in their craft, but if their skill goes no further than the utilitarian, they are not generally described as artisans. Likewise, the sculptor and the fine painter may be gifted artists and create great works in their turn, but artists create with little or no regard for the usefulness of their work. Instead, they are concerned solely with the aesthetic of the thing – they too, are not described as artisans. Only when these two principles come together do we recognise the true artisan. The artisan creates for utility, which means for service, but also with an equal eye to the aesthetic of the piece.

So the artisan is concerned with beauty, but a beauty that is broader and deeper than the concern of the artist. To the artisan, beauty extends beyond the beauty of form to include the entire character of the work created, which includes beauty of function, or as I have said, beauty of service.

Depending on the purpose of the work, beauty can sometimes be more prominent in service. For example, a violin may have an aesthetic beauty, but its greater beauty lies in its ability to produce music in the skilled hands of a fine musician – it has a beauty of character that derives from its service more than its appearance. This is not to diminish the beauty of form, which also contributes to the character of the piece. And the artisan achieves his most excellent and beautiful work when there is beauty in both.

Now, this desire, this effort, to realise the beautiful within their work, is evident to all who behold it, but what the beholder cannot know is the love the artisan has for the work itself. I do not mean simply the process, as when we say of such a man that he loves what he does, that he puts himself into his work, or has a passion for his work. These things are true in a sense, but they are merely the detached and slightly euphemistic ways of describing a love that is actual and real for the work itself. I say euphemistic because there is something awkward, even self-conscious, about loving the object of one's own creation. And for the majority, it is a love not generally experienced at any high or conscious level, and therefore, it is hard to communicate without the risk of misunderstanding.

Even when it does exist, it is not obvious because its object is soulless and therefore incapable of acknowledging such a love; that is, it lacks the relational dimension and is consequently less well defined than the love of a mother for her child, for instance. But this does not make it less real, it simply means it lacks the opportunity for expression, whereas, by contrast, a mother's love is observed daily through the back-and-forth interactions within a relationship.

But even for a mother's love, a relationship is not prerequisite. A mother's love is no less real if her love is unrequited or unknown to her child. For example, by the very strength of her love, the mother who has given up her child to preserve a life for it away from some danger – perhaps in time of war – does not cease to love the child; she will love the child as long as she lives. Her love is not made any the less, or less real, even if the child grows up in a foreign country far from all knowledge of the mother. The mother's love exists whether or not there is a relationship. Similarly, the love of the artisan is not made less real because the object of his creation cannot know his love. It is only less obvious, less observed.

But if this kind of love is not, by and large, part of the general consciousness, it is not for that reason absent entirely from our experience. Whether conscious of it or not, most of us have experienced this *artisian* love, even if it is faint and indistinct, and we do not recognise it for what it is.

It can be mistaken for joy, or delight, or even satisfaction. It is felt more keenly at an early age, perhaps, by the child who builds castles in the sand or who paints, but it can remain through all the various stages of life – though it is subtle, and without humility, it is easily lost to pride.

But the true artisan has spent a lifetime in his craft, and even if there is still the temptation of pride, this *artisan* love is at least more obvious to his own mind. And if humility has, by discipline, become his habit, it is a love that grows more distinct over time, to the point where the artisan recognises it for what it is – not simply delight or satisfaction, but genuine love.

However, there is something this sort of love is not. We should be careful not to conflate it with devotion, where, in this context, devotion implies service to the thing created. That would be an inversion of the intent of the artisan and hence, a corruption of that love.

Devotion also implies value inherent, immanent, in the work itself but the artisan, of all people, is safe from making that mistake. He is only too aware of the labour required to produce the finished article where, if there is any value in it at all, its value has been imparted into the piece by the artisan. Thus, its value has been created independently from itself and therefore, the genesis of its value is not immanent in the work – others may worship the idol, but never the man who fashions it.

The Artisan

That the artisan is not devoted to his work can also be seen at any stage in the work's progress. For example, with work already begun, and through no fault of his own, a defect may be discovered that puts the whole project at risk. Perhaps a piece of wood, under the plane or chisel, reveals a previously undetected flaw only after the surface wood has been pared away. If this should occur, he can sometimes repair the defect or modify his design to work around it. However, if the defect is irremediable, the value in his work has been erased entirely; in which case, it will be discarded or even consigned to the fire for burning.

Further, its value is not immutable even when the work has been completed. Its value remains only if the work continues to be useful for its intended service, even if it has already seen many years in that service. For example, if the piece is broken through some mishap and becomes useless for its purpose, it is good for nothing; again, it is thrown out and burned.

So, while it is true that the artisan values his work, he does not see that value as immanent in the thing itself. Therefore, however we describe the artisan's love of the work he creates, it is not the love of devotion, however much it is valued.

Yet, the love of the artisan is a love that does recognize value in his work; only, as I have said, it is a value imparted, not immanent. From where does this value come, then?

Perhaps, the easy answer is that the artisan perceives its value as simply a reflection of his own – that any and all value comes from the artisan himself. But if the artisan's skill imparts some value, surely it goes too far to say all the value in the work is the result of his skill. There is at least a collaboration in the materials he uses; the metals have been mined and refined by others, and the wood has been harvested with much labour before his turn. One could go further and say that God ultimately created them all.

The artisan knows this, and to assume the artisan sees the genesis of his work's value in himself is the easy, but false, assumption of the novice or the uninitiated, who do not have the artisan's experience or self-awareness. The artisan knows more keenly than anyone that his skill is not self-made, but through a tangible and often laborious process, has itself been made, and made in himself. And because he knows this through experience, he is more likely to view himself simply as a partner in a greater collaboration.

Thus, the artisan no more finds the genesis of the value of his work in himself than he does in the object

The Artisan

he is fashioning. This means the artisan recognises value in his work in a much more objective sense than is commonly assumed, and as something largely independent from himself.

We draw closer to the reason the work has value to the artisan when we consider the extent to which the work fulfils his intent. In the eyes of the artisan, value is closely connected to its service – how well the work serves his purpose and whether there is beauty in that service. These are the things that are valuable to the artisan, and if there is any lack there, then the value of the work, in his eyes, is likewise diminished. To say that another way, the artisan only perceives value in his work in so far as he achieves the beautiful – by which, again, I mean beauty of character, which includes the beauty of service.

There is, then, a higher principle at play here, a principle greater than the artisan himself, and by which, he can judge objectively whether his work is truly beautiful in the broader sense I have described. That standard, or principle, is the principle of the good. For it is from the good in the work he fashions that any beauty in his work ultimately derives. The artisan asks: is it good, and good for service?

Beauty, to the artisan, is merely this higher principle of the good made manifest and observed; as clothing is the adornment of the body or as actions are the reflection of the soul. If the artisan can love the work he creates, it is only because he seeks the good, and recognises that good made visible in, and through, the work he has fashioned. It is the good that makes his work beautiful, and valuable, and worthy of his love, because at its pith, the love of the artisan is a love of all that is good – because it is a love of the good.

If the author's attempt at describing the artisan is, in some ways, an idealised picture, it is not overly so. The life of the artisan has been the author's daily experience for all his working life, and it is from that long experience, and not his imagination, that it is here set forth – it has not been stretched beyond what the author's own experience will allow.

But that experience is not common to everyone. It is not like the universal experience of fatherhood; where, even if all are not fathers, nevertheless, all understand and have known what fatherhood is. Even those who have not known a personal father have an implicit understanding of what it should be, and almost always can point to 'father figures' in their own lives – those who can often be better examples of fatherhood itself.

However, the true experience of the artisan is generally confined to relatively few in our modern societies. Consequently, it is not an idea near to the general consciousness, and therefore, this *artisian* love is not easily recognised or appreciated for what it is. But if it is farther from our consciousness than the metaphors of the husband and father, it is not for that reason farther from the truth it seeks to describe; it is, in fact, much closer to that truth.

Like all metaphors, it is not the whole truth, but it orbits about the truth. If metaphors like the father and the husband track in more or less circular orbits like the planets, the metaphor of the artisan tracks in the extreme, elongated ellipse of the comet. It remains distant and outside our field of view for long stretches of time. However, unlike the planets, when it does at last appear, it approaches closer to that truth, and it burns all the brighter.

It approaches closer because it emphasises the fundamental relation between God and man – that of the Creator to His creation – and it keeps that relation in the foreground of our thought at all times. And it represents an *authority* both real and absolute, and it is not an authority in any sense shared by consent or otherwise, as might be suggested by the marriage metaphor. Neither is it the authority of the governor; that is, the authority of a father.

Of course, there is another metaphor that approaches that absolute authority: the authority of the sovereign monarch. But even the authority of a king is not absolute. Yes, a king can take a life, he can even spare a life by his own decree, but it is not in his power to create life.

What these metaphors have in common is the way they represent different types of *authority*, but always an authority between those of the same kind; their commonality is in humanity itself.

That is not the case for the metaphor of the artisan, which introduces an 'otherness' to the relation, representing an authority between uniquely different kinds. This 'otherness' puts the artisan in a unique, and primary category, whereas the metaphors of father, husband, and king are at most secondary.

The artisan alone has an *absolute* authority to create for his own pleasure and purpose. The raw material in his hand has no commonality about it that might afford it a right or voice in the process. There is an 'otherness' that admits of no consultation as to what it will become or for what purpose it is intended, and it is precisely this 'otherness' that allows the metaphor of the artisan to approach closer to the reality it seeks to convey, because it represents better, the primary idea of the absolute authority of God.

CHAPTER V

THE ARTISAN
PART II

HE PRIMARY IDEA of absolute authority in the metaphor of the artisan moves us closer to our true relation to the Creator. But though important, it is simply the foundation, and it does not, by itself, tell us anything more about the *character* of our Creator, or His love toward His creatures.

As I have previously said, Creator, is an absolute title; it can only be held exclusively, by one unique Being. It reveals an absolute truth, but a truth that is somewhat cold; it is silent with regard to the idea of the moral. That can leave us despairing of any hope of understanding, or of connection with such a Being.

But the metaphor of the artisan speaks to us of the Creator's *Personhood*, and in a primary sense, because unlike other metaphors, it is built upon a foundation of absolute authority. And like the title, Creator, the

The Purposeful Love of God

metaphor of the artisan represents a special relation between different kinds, but it represents that 'otherness', and the absolute authority that goes with it, in such a way that does not diminish the idea of the moral. Rather, the absolute authority of the artisan retains a moral character that is not lost to that authority, but rules over it – and at the same time asserts and elevates it. It is the *personhood* of the artisan that translates that absolute authority into an absolute *moral* authority.

That is a direct inference from personhood, for to be a person is to be a moral being. And by moral, I mean that at the centre of every person, it is the moral will that rules all else; that is, our actions, thoughts, desires, hopes, interests, loves, hates – in short, all that makes us truly a person – are centred in our moral will, and it is from that centre we live.

I will go further and say that the artisan takes that idea of personhood and gives it *personality*, which means it makes that personhood *unique*. As a metaphor for God, it shapes everything about His Person and makes it His own: actions, thoughts, desires, hopes, interests, love, hate – they are all modified into something uniquely personal to His own identity. These things take on *His* identity, and therefore, whatever commonality they have with humanity, they nevertheless possess their own *unique* moral character.

The Artisan

❧

To return to the metaphor proper, there are several things that can be said regarding the personhood of the artisan. The first is that what he creates must necessarily be fashioned to some standard, which, because the artisan is a person, means a moral standard. Furthermore, that moral standard reflects his own *personality* – it is *his* moral standard.

I am not, for now, concerned with what that standard is – that is not my point. It makes little difference whether that standard comes from an authority outside, or above himself, if it has been subsumed to his own moral identity. The point is that it is *personal* to himself – it is who he is, and that he cannot create apart from his own moral personality.

That is an important point because it helps us understand why, for the artisan, it matters very little whether his work is valued by others, if it does not first meet his own standards. It is a matter of *personal* integrity and honour because each piece is, in some small, but real sense, a reflection of what *he* calls good and beautiful. Therefore, he will not permit anything to leave his workshop unless, and until, it meets his standards.

A second point follows from the first and expands on it. It is that everything he makes must inevitably be, in some way, and to some degree, also a reflection of his personality. This includes his moral standard, but it is much more than that; it points us toward his own interests, tastes, and loves. These things are what might be called the *positive* expression of his personality.

That is not to say that his character can be fully known through his works. It is often more to the point that it is only those who have first truly come to know him personally who, because of that experience, can then recognise his personality in the pieces he has made. Perhaps it is enough to say that we find in his works, *shadows* of his true character; certainly, we do not see any contradiction to that character.

The parallels are obvious. God is also a moral personality, and therefore He does not create in a moral vacuum. Everything He creates springs from His own unique moral personality, which means, of course, those things He likes and values – the positive expression of His personality – but also those things He does not, for personality encompasses both.

Further, He fashions all that He makes to His own moral standard; what He calls the beautiful and the good. And it cannot be that He should allow anything that bears His signature to be anything less than His standard allows, and that standard is high indeed – that, at least, is plain.

But what follows, because His authority is absolute,

is that what God is making will, without doubt or compromise, also be fully realised. There is nothing in heaven or on earth – neither principalities nor powers, nor the wickedness or sin of man, or angels – that can stand against the completion of what He has begun.

His work will also not fail in its *character* to be beautiful itself; by which, I mean not simply its form but also its beauty of service. It will all, to the last tiny detail, be finished and made complete to His own holy standard – the standard of *His* good. And when His great work with humanity is finally realised in its perfection, the record will once more show that, "God saw all that He had made, and behold, it was very good."*

For that statement is not limited to the original creative act. It reaches out prophetically to the completion of His great work with humanity – the summing up of all things in Christ – as an absolute pronouncement that all He has made is very good. And it is because it is good that it is beautiful, valuable, and worthy of His love.

However, on the face of it, that seems to be a denial of our present reality, and to suggest that this is the attitude of God toward humanity is not easy for many to accept. Indeed, some sections of the church believe God

---

* Gen 1:31

loves us only against His better judgment; that there is nothing in humanity worthy of His love and that He must love only because it is His nature.

There have been misguided – and largely successful – attempts by some theologians to codify this belief into Christian orthodoxy by redefining the very idea of God's love. Thus, they speak of the love of God as incomprehensible and even irrational. They say His love is not only unmerited but also unmotivated because there can be no value, nothing good, in creation that could possibly justify or motivate His love. But the far greater sin is in their attempt to take the Greek word, *agape*, and strip it of all historical connection from a love of the worthy, and instead make it to mean precisely the opposite: God's love of the worthless.

The irony in this thinking is that it comes from a sincere, though misguided, attempt to magnify God's love. It seeks to emphasise the vast gulf between mankind and God, and to show thereby, as they suppose, the infinite greatness of the love that reaches across it. But their method to achieve this is simply to attempt to reduce man to the lowest level by declaring him unlovable – which, in the end, is nothing but a meaningless and ineffectual subtraction, and it merely exposes a poor grasp of mathematics. For between the finite and the infinite, there is no subtraction – or addition, multiplication, or any other operation – that can alter in the slightest degree, the magnitude of the

The Artisan

moral relation that separates God the Creator from His creation.

This way of thinking is really the old Gnosticism, raising its head in the church once more. And it is as false today as it was then because it cuts directly across what God Himself has done in making man in His own image. In so doing, He raised man to a place higher than even the angels. Indeed, He has raised him as high as is divinely possible, and it is never wise to attempt to make less of what God has done, much less try to undo it.

The fault in such thinking does not lie in recognising the gulf between God and His creation, or in its attempt to take sin seriously. That is only too real and near to our experience to deny. Rather, the fault lies in its myopic imagination that can see nothing but what is immediately in front of it. It perceives the constant wearing away and ruin of water upon rock, but sees not the majestic beauty of the cascading waterfall – it lacks the imagination that can survey the surrounding country. But God sees it all, and sees it altogether, as one, because its purpose in Him is one, and there is no part of all His creation that does not serve that purpose, not even a frail and broken humanity.

If God made the physical universe in seven days and then rested, He did not rest for long. He is at work still, except that He now works in the moral dimension on the hearts of men. Mankind is a work in progress, and if 'it has not appeared as yet what we shall be', when His

The Purposeful Love of God

work is finally finished, we shall realise that what we thought was all ruin and sin, was simply one more tool in His hand, used with the superior skill of the Artisan to serve His end from the very beginning. God sees that country – and declares it not just good, but very good.

※

However, it is here that we come up against at least one insufficiency in the metaphor of the artisan. If the metaphor of an earthly father can go too far, the weakness in the metaphor of the artisan is in the opposite direction – it does not go far enough. If the artisan can love what he has made because it is good, how much more does God love the work of His own creation because, unlike the artisan, He *is* the good. Everything He creates springs from His own goodness, or to use the language of religion, from holiness.

The aphorism, 'God loves because He is love', might be sufficient for the child in Sunday School, but if that is where the child's faith remains, it will never attain to a mature faith. When John says, "God is *agape*",[*] he does not leave us to assume the kind of love that suits our own sentiment, but he goes on to describe that love as propitiatory, through the death of God's only begotten Son. That is, John juxtaposes that love with the real,

---

[*] 1 Jn 4:8

and very personal, wrath of God. In so doing, he ties that love to holiness; or better, to God's holy *personality*. Thus, John defines God's love by God's *character* – by who He is – and not the other way around.

It is from holiness – His essential personality – that He creates what is good and beautiful, and therefore, delights in, values, and loves, the works He has made.

It may be in God's nature to love, but that is not the same as saying His character has everything to do with love. He is no more a slave to His love than He is a slave to His wrath. He rules them both by His own moral will, they are both the *expression* of His holy personality – one positive, the other negative, but each as much a part of who He is as the other.

The metaphor of the father is too close to our experience to see this. We need to stand outside, farther away from our experience, to see His reality more objectively. The metaphor of the artisan allows us to do this because, being closer to His reality, it is farther from our own. Through the metaphor, we see His love has little to do with any quality immanent in man and everything to do with *His* character.

This leads us back to the idea of value. We have seen the artisan has a love of the good, and his intent is to see that good manifest in the works he creates – what he perceives as beauty. Again, this beauty is more than the aesthetic; it is the beauty of *character*. And value, as the artisan sees it, is found only in so far as his work realises the beautiful.

Similarly, God finds value in the works He has made, except the standard by which He judges that beauty lies within Himself. This means the character He looks for in His work is simply His own. In other words, God finds value in His creation precisely *because* it bears the imprint of His own character, and if there is any good in creation, in humanity, it is because it is the reflection of His own goodness. That is what He values, and that is what inspires and motivates His love.

Thus, the metaphor of the artisan draws us back to an ancient idea, an idea some have forgotten, and others have unwittingly tried to erase from the love of God. It is the idea, rare among men and therefore rare in speech, but at one time conveyed by the Greek word, *agape*. It is the idea of a love that is motivated and inspired by what is good, and therefore valuable, in the object of that love.

It is the kind of love we see in the love of the artisan for his work, and if this love is rare among men, it is not so with God. It is this old *agape* love, or, if I may be permitted, this *artisan* love, that is present in His love for all that He has made. And it is especially there where John says, "For God so loved the world". And it is the only real answer to the question: "why?"

CHAPTER VI

STEADFAST LOVE

F GOD FINDS value in His creation because it bears the imprint of His own character, the corollary is: if the works of God do not have that beauty of character, then to the same extent, they have lost value in His eyes. And if, say, in the course of manufacture, this beauty of character should be corrupted or lost, then the value of that work has been lost altogether, and consequently ceases to be the object of His love – it is fit only to be thrown out and burned.

Surely then, this is the actual situation of the race, and the doom that hangs over us. For mankind may still, in some vague sense, bear His image, but it has long since ceased to reflect His character. And this raises the question: why has our doom not already fallen?

Actually, it came very close in the days of Noah. It was at that time in history, more than any other, that God debated whether to continue with the work He had begun with humanity, or to scrap it altogether. Except for Noah and his family, eight persons in all, it might have gone very differently, but at that time God decided to persevere and continue His work with the race of men a while longer.

It is worth pointing out that even if He had chosen the destruction of the entire race, it would not necessarily have signalled the abandonment of His overall goal. The realisation of His overarching purpose and design would not fail – even the destruction of the entire race could be no hindrance to that end. The only question was whether His purpose could still be realised using the raw material presently in His hand, or whether humanity would be discarded entirely, and the work begun again with altogether new material. So, down through the history of men, we observe God's perseverance, and implicit within that perseverance, a love that is real, steadfast, and constant.

This is the great theme of the Old Testament, so often written and celebrated in the Psalms. And perhaps, no one else could have written it better than David, for it was said of him that he was a man after God's own heart; though at times his actions were the antithesis of that statement – and David saw the contradiction and felt it keenly.

Still, God forgave his sin, and His love was an

abiding presence in his life. And David's gratitude and wonder poured out into his psalms, proclaiming a love he knew by experience to be steadfast, and by the Spirit, to be everlasting.

Yet, for all the assurance David found in God, he did not consider God's love something guaranteed to everyone; it was a steadfast, but not an indiscriminate, love.

> "But the lovingkindness of the LORD is from everlasting to everlasting *on those who fear Him* ".*
> (Ps 103:17)

That is no statement of universal or unconditional love – though it should be noted that it does not make that condition some high standard of righteousness, but rather the attitude of the contrite; that is, it rested on those of a particular *character* and not those of a certain sinlessness.

With that insight, David was a man ahead of his time, but even for David, it was not a love guaranteed to all. Neither did it exist somehow independently from God's own interest.

---

* Emphasis added

The Purposeful Love of God

> "The LORD will fulfill his purpose for me;
> your steadfast love, O LORD, endures forever.
> Do not forsake the work of your hands."
> (Ps 138:8, ESV)

David saw God's work and purpose in his own life, and he understood that God's love was bound up with that purpose. God's love was active in the work God was doing, and therefore, like that work, it would also endure. This had profound implications for David, for it meant that if God's love was an enduring love, then he, as the object of that love, must also endure – even beyond the grave.

> "For You will not abandon my soul to Sheol;
> Nor will You allow Your Holy One to undergo decay.
> You will make known to me the path of life;
> In Your presence is fullness of joy;
> In Your right hand there are pleasures forever."
> (Ps 16:10-11)

David's profound experience of God raised his eyes

far beyond his own place in history to see far into the future – into eternity. This was in no small part because the nature of that love could not be rationalised within the limited framework of his own finite life.

But he saw further, and perceived an overarching, and what is more, an *everlasting* purpose, focused on something far grander and more significant than his own temporal need. And because he was caught up in that purpose, in like manner he was also caught up in that love – and he was swept along by it as if in the current of a mighty river.

But upon what, exactly, was that love focused? If that question seems strange, it is because it is seldom, if ever, asked. And it is not asked because the answer is assumed to be self-evident. God's love is focused on humanity: "for God so loved the world", we supply in answer – and it is quite true. The church has always found the answer there, whenever it has asked the question.

Only, that answer is to see God's love from our own interest – it is a view too self-occupied with our own need to ponder whether that love might include, and even serve, the interest of God.

But David's life, if it was anything, was a testimony to the interest of God. God had taken him from the sheep and set him as king over God's people. It was something done by God, and for His own purpose and interest.

David understood this and knew that his well-being and more, his very life, were wrapped up in that overarching interest. Therefore, even when his need was the most extreme, he would press God's purposes in his prayers, as the argument most likely to prevail and persuade, because David understood it was only as he was included in God's great work that he himself would endure.

And so it is with all the race of men. God's love may rest upon individuals and even on the world, but it does so only as it is part of His purpose and work.

Not all will be saved. It is not even that most will be – at least if Jesus' words are to be taken seriously.

"For many are called, but few are chosen."
(Matt 22:14)

Much is being pared away as His work progresses, and the shavings lie plentiful upon the workshop floor. There they lie for the moment, but when His work is complete, the floor will be swept and the rubbish burned, before His finished work is displayed in glory.

That so many should be lost, like discarded shavings

upon the workshop floor, might be seen as a failure on God's part, and a failure of the cross, except that the salvation of the entire race and its sinlessness was never God's principal goal.

A sinless humanity might, perhaps, have been realised if Adam and Eve had chosen differently, but even in that case, He was making something far more significant than merely a sinless race. He is focused upon, and works towards, completing a work so much greater than that – a work of beauty and of a particular character far beyond the foundational prerequisite of righteousness. A work which, as likely as not, is produced more effectively through a process of attrition, rather than through any additive process alone.

To view, as David did, God's steadfast love from *His* interest is an essential step toward spiritual maturity. And that is a statement that does not reflect well upon the maturity of the church today, which seems to be obsessed with all things to do with ourselves: our blessing, our need, our joy, and our happiness. But that is the immaturity of the child. The question is whether the maturity of the church has come much farther when it considers God's entire interest to be: our salvation, our sanctification, our sinlessness, our holiness and charity? Those things are higher ideals, to be sure, but the focus is still in the same direction. Is that not simply a subtle and more refined immaturity, made so by the implicit assumption that God's interest is still occupied, only and always, with ourselves?

The church has done the same thing with the love of God. It has taken the revelation of God's love for the world and assumed it is *all* of God's love; that is, it has come to consider God's focus upon the fallen race as the sum total of His interest.

But that, again, is the narrow immaturity of the child who, surrounded by the love of parents, is blinded by the affirmation it gives and cannot imagine beyond its own needs to consider the broader interests of its parents. Only when the child grows and is confronted by some experience of the parent, independent from themselves, often of loss or pain, does the child begin to consider the parent's interests.

Along those same lines, we can ask: does the love of God for the world really exhaust all of God's interest? Is that really the sum total of His personality?

When that question is finally asked, the self-centredness of such an assumption becomes plain. And it is the cross, above all, that brings it home. For it is there that we finally see *His* burden and suffering. But it is only when that suffering is seen as God *acting*, not simply on behalf of the race but for His *own* interest, and the church rises beyond herself to consider what the cross accomplished for Himself, that she takes a more meaningful step toward maturity.

> "He died for all, so that they who live might no longer live for themselves, but for Him who died and rose again on their behalf."
> (2 Cor 5: 15)

To see the steadfast love of God from the point of view of God's interest, is to understand that its focus is toward something beyond the individual's immediate need, as it is also beyond the collective need of the race.

Yes, God is concerned with our need, which means, chiefly, our redemption and reconciliation to God, for these things are necessary for our everlasting life. But though the cross met our need it did not exhaust all the purpose and power of that supreme sacrifice. As momentous as these things are for the race, in the end, they are merely prerequisites to our participation in His own greater interest, and even our redemption is secured to meet *His* interest.

As He fashions us according to His own requirements, God meets our tremendous and desperate need, but He does so, as it were, in passing – and we are swept up in His train, on the way to a destination that is the fulfilment of His great purpose and interest. That is where His focus lies, and if His love is steadfast, it is steadfast towards that end.

The real service and value of the metaphor of the artisan is that it emphasises that end. It lifts us beyond our own interest and reveals the interest of God.

CHAPTER VII

EVERLASTING LOVE

THE METAPHOR OF the artisan can make us aware of the interest of God, but like all metaphors, it has its limits. From the metaphor, we understand the artisan has a perception of the object he is working on, which is dependent upon where, in time, that process happens to be. At the beginning of his work, the material has comparatively little value, and it is not until its completion that its value is fully realised. His motivation may be a love for the good, but the good he labours towards is only achieved when the work is finished; only then does the object become valuable in his eyes and therefore, worthy of love.

By contrast, the love David spoke about was already mature, already everlasting, when the object of that love was neither. Thus, it seems we have reached a point where the metaphor is found to be somewhat insufficient; it does not reflect the presence of God's full and mature love for His object, when that object is not

The Purposeful Love of God

finished and has not yet realised the good that inspires such love. Which is to say, contrary to the metaphor, God's love appears to precede its own reason to exist.

That a difficulty should arise is not surprising because a metaphor is seldom accurate on all points. It is usually enough if a metaphor approaches accuracy on the central point it seeks to convey. However, the difference just highlighted cannot be quickly ignored because it is acutely relevant to our central theme on a fundamental level.

The reason the metaphor fails at this point is that all metaphors taken from the world are necessarily constrained to the normal flow of time within history. They are simply too anthropomorphic when applied to the God of eternity; by which, I mean they can only represent actions within our framework of time, with all the presuppositions that attach to that. And those presuppositions are unlikely to hold for an eternal God, for whom time has little relevance.

I am aware that this may seem unnecessarily philosophical because today, the temptation is to dismiss philosophy as solely an academic pursuit, with little relevance or impact on the practical man; I mean the man caught up with living, with work and play – the man with neither the time nor the inclination toward such things.

And there are two things to be said about this. The first is that such a man is not nearly practical enough, and the second is that true philosophy has little to do with academic pursuit, but is in fact, first and foremost, practical.

David was such a man. He was a shepherd in his youth, and in his responsibility to protect the flock, he fought and killed both the bear and the lion. He later became a soldier, skilled in sling, sword, and bow, and he would go on to command the armies of Israel, and eventually become king. Yet, despite a life filled with such practicalities, or perhaps because of them, he also became the great psalmist and philosopher of Israel.

But his was not the philosophy of the academic, who can keep separate the speculative thought of his discipline from the practicalities of life. For David, his thoughts were the reasoned consequence of the practical hardships and contradictions that engulfed him – especially during those desperate years in which he was hunted by Saul.

Those were years, often in fear for his life, that brought the more profound questions of time and eternity to his waking thought. Rather than driving them from his mind, his circumstances intensified their importance, and through the hardships of his experience, his faith took on a more disciplined and practical understanding. With that gained understanding, coupled with faith, he found the courage to face the challenges and contradictions in his own life.

For instance, by faith and testimony, he knew that God loved and delighted in him, even while his life hung in the balance. Through faith, he came to understand that, in the end, God's love and his life were connected; either the extinguishing of his mortal life would bring that eternal love to naught, or else God's love must swallow up his mortality in a life everlasting.

And David took God's side, as he always did, because he saw that his own history was a participation in the interest of God – and he knew that God's interest would not fail. Therefore, however absurd it must have seemed, he concluded that as an object of His love, his own life must necessarily endure beyond the grave.

That is a tremendous insight, and it is, of all things, the most practical. But David did not stop there. Seeing himself caught up in the interest of God, he saw his own history extending into eternity in *both* directions – from everlasting to everlasting.

David began to see his own history not only from God's interest, but also from God's *perspective*. The result was that David could project his own history, not simply into the eternal future but also into the eternal past – beyond his own experience certainly, but not beyond the experience of God.

> "Your eyes have seen my unformed substance;
> And in Your book were all written
> The days that were ordained for me,
> When as yet there was not one of them."
> (Ps 139:16)

Those verses are no formal statement of predestination. David was not concerned with the academic philosophy or theology of it. He was, as I have said, interested in practicalities, which means he was interested in history, because history, if it is anything, represents the things that are solid, tangible, real, matter-of-fact; which is to say, practical. But to consider how his own history might appear to an eternal God lead him back before his own beginning in history, to a prior time in God's eternity.

David saw time like a number line, stretched into the distant past and future. God was above that line and could view the future as easily as the past, yet history itself was still something that played out relative to time; that is, he saw history as a series of events, the one following the other, with its flow always in the forward direction. God could see the future, but the events of history all necessarily projected forward.

That is not entirely inaccurate – there is doubtless

order even in eternity. But David was no modern; he had not the benefit of a modern science that raises questions about the nature of time itself.

Thus his thinking represents a beginning, and a strong beginning, but it is still tied to our own human experience from within the flow of time, and it is unlikely that our experience translates into eternity without some qualification. To point this out is not to dismiss David's view but to draw attention to the seldom conscious presuppositions of our own experience, which can lead us to conclusions that do not necessarily apply to an eternal God.

For instance, if we limit ourselves to this view of history, it is a natural conclusion that historical events can only impact what follows those events. That is, an event in time cannot impact whatever has preceded it; an event can only affect the present and the future, if it has any impact at all. That might seem obvious, but it is only obvious because of presuppositions held, based on our experience within the framework of time.

However, it is not obvious that history should have the same flow from God's perspective. For God, time itself has a beginning, and therefore if God is above time, it is in a wholly different sense than just described.

What that means in terms of physics is anybody's guess; that is the question of relativity, which, as interesting as it is, it is not what I am driving at. The point I wish to make is not with respect to the relativity of time, but with respect to the *relevancy* of time to an eternal God.

For our purposes, it is enough to note that time does not have the same *relevance* to God as it does to all those who live and move within it. And because time has little relevance to God, He does not view history in the same way His creation does – with the same flow and direction – which means, for God, the efficacy of the events in history do not necessarily affect only what comes after them but, possibly, also what came before.

For an eternal God, it is history that matters most, not time, because history is where time touches eternity, and vice versa; an intersection through *action* and not through thought alone.

Nowhere is this intersection more manifest than at the cross, that terrible and glorious moment in history that changed everything forever.

> "But now once at the consummation of the ages He has been manifested to put away sin by the sacrifice of Himself."
> (Heb 9:26)

It may be beyond our reach to understand how an eternal God exists outside, or above time, but His *action* through the cross, in history, occurred only once, whether in time or eternity. It may have been appointed for a specific time in history, but that is incidental to the fact itself. What mattered, both to God and man, was not *when* it was done but *that* it was done; it is the fact, the *history* of it, that matters most. And if the action of the cross changed the course of our history, it more profoundly changed eternity – and changed it in an instant, and altogether.

Perhaps one way to picture the enormity of that change is to think of eternity, not as infinite time but as infinite space, with the historic action of the cross viewed as an explosion of light from a single source, which radiates out instantaneously in all directions; it fills that space and changes all of it forever. It was that source, the singularity of the cross, the history of it, that mattered, and mattered once and for all.

To an eternal God, that event might not, strictly speaking, have a beginning in time, but that does not mean it did not have an origin in the space of eternity – even if what that means practically, is only known to God who holds eternity in His hand.

And this leads us to the idea that the cross has, in some sense, a history within eternity. Thus, John can say of the resurrected Jesus, that he appeared, "a Lamb standing, as if slain."*

John is not simply memorialising that event in

---

* Rev 5:6

history, but he is making reference to the full power and eternal efficacy of the cross which fills eternity now and always; that is, eternity itself was changed by that historic event.

If that is a difficult concept, it at least has a history that flows in the familiar, forward direction. When John, later in the same book, says essentially the same thing, "the Lamb slain from the foundation of the world",* that is an idea significantly more challenging to grasp.

But John was not trying to be difficult; it was not even that he was being mystical. Certainly, he does not mean that Jesus had already died before He walked the shores of Galilee, and the cross would eventually catch up with that death in history. No, his meaning is the same as before. In both cases, John, in the Spirit, sees that singular event from outside time, with all the natural perspective of the Divine; only, the first phrase matches our familiar human perspective, while the second flows in the opposite direction.

Neither is it a reference to the foreknowledge or omniscience of God. Those are valuable constructs in their place, but they do suffer from the same anthropomorphic bent. It is not that God, in His omniscience, reached out through time, with foreknowledge, before the world was made, and therefore knew that His Son would die on that cross. Instead, it was that God, above time, was in eternity – an eternity *already changed* in its entirety by

---

* Rev 13:8, NKJV

that singular event in history.

For all who live within time today, that event appeared in history over two thousand years ago, and to those who are being saved, the cross is the power of God to all who believe. The church looks back to that historical event, memorialising it in the sacrament of the bread and wine. The fact of the cross in history, and its memorial, fit the natural flow of time, but the power of that great sacrifice on the cross has filled all eternity, which includes from before the foundation of the world.

That is no mere philosophical statement. With respect to the salvation of the race, it is entirely practical. It means the salvation made possible by the cross is available and *effectual* for the entire race – whether men lived before that event in time, or after it.

Thus, Jesus can say, "I am the way, and the truth, and the life; *no one* comes to the Father but through Me."[*]

❦

The church has always seen in the Old Testament, a *foreshadowing* of the cross – from the clothing of Adam and Eve with the skins of animals, to the sacrifice of Isaac by his father, to the Passover lamb of Egypt, to all the various sacrifices of the Jewish cultus. It is undoubtedly and obviously so, though it is only obvious after the fact.

---

[*] Jn 14:6 (Emphasis added)

But it may be more accurate to say these things were all, from God's perspective, a *memorial* of the cross, every bit as immanent and present to the eternal God as the bread and the wine; not pointing forward to a future time but *memorialising* something already real in the history of eternity. In that sense, the cross was already effectual, from when Adam first sinned, and so on all down through the natural history of the world.

That is not to say that those who experienced the forgiveness of God saw it that way. For instance, the Jews did not really have a well-formed understanding of the rationale of their sacrifices; they offered them from obedience and faith. None of the Jewish worshippers could have conceived the reality of the cross in history. Neither were they expected to. They had no reference in history to gauge the magnitude of the cost of their forgiveness; no comparable or definitive event or act, to which they could trace back to its source, so mighty a river. Yet, they felt its power nonetheless and, by faith, knew their forgiveness to be real and effectual.

And the forgiveness, nay, the salvation they obtained through faith, was in no wise different from our own, because its source was not in the sacrifice and blood of goats, but in the eternal efficacy of the cross.

The Purposeful Love of God

Yet, without any specific act in history to hang their experience upon, it must have seemed – as in fact, it did seem to David – that the source of that forgiveness, and the love it revealed, had neither beginning nor end. It was, to use his own words, a love from everlasting to everlasting. His mercies were new every morning, with a love that filled all eternity and all time, and was, in the truest sense, eternal.

But that is to perceive God's love through the *experience* of faith, which is *our* point of contact – eternity reaching across and touching us within time. But however real that experience is to the race, however obvious that might seem, it is still, in the end, a perception from within our perspective in time. And it is not obvious that it should appear the same from God's perspective in eternity. For all David's insight and genius, it was but a beginning. He could go so far, and no farther, because the foundation of that forgiveness had not yet been revealed in history – it was still hidden, or at best, scarcely implied. It would be the church's privilege, who now live in the light of the enormity of the historic cross, to make the foundation of that forgiveness explicit in the death and resurrection of Christ.

That is why John can say what he does. John sees the action of God in the historic cross as the source, the fountainhead, from which flows God's forgiveness to the whole world.

Thus, it is John who leads us back to the idea of an *origin*, or in some sense, a beginning of God's forgiveness in eternity. And to approach it from the other direction would be to say, the cross, for John, is the focal point of all redemptive history, regardless of where, in time, it is viewed. Indeed, that is to see things more from God's side where that fountainhead, that beginning, springs not from sentiment, or hope, or thought alone, but from an *action* on God's part, as real in eternity as it is in history – something completed, something finished, something done.

The Purposeful Love of God

CHAPTER VIII

THE BEGINNING OF GOD'S LOVE

OD'S LOVE FOR the world is as old as the world itself, but is it accurate to say it began there, at the creation of that world? David describes God's love as being from everlasting to everlasting, so to speak of a beginning seems to be a contradiction on the face of it. And some recoil from the very idea of a beginning on principle; it implies, as they suppose, something less than eternal and therefore something limited – less than perfect, less than God. But that is just too neat to be real; it employs a logic too narrow, which leaves no place for personality.

A God who limits Himself by His own will may be more faithful to Himself – that is, to His own moral personality – than if He remained inert, unmoved, lest He offend those who insist upon a stricter logic. And in any case, that stricter logic is of no use when it comes to the idea of moral perfection – and with God, it is the moral that is supreme.

I shall have more to say about perfection later, but it is enough to say in passing that God did so limit Himself when He took the form of man and brought that form into Godhead – not for a season, but for all eternity. With that act, He showed His contempt for that neat and logical, but ultimately irrelevant form of perfection, as He rose to the heedless extravagance of the hallowing of His own moral personality.

But I digress, it is not the nature of God and His capacity to love that is here in view. Instead, it is His love *for the world*, along with the question of whether that love might be said to have a beginning, in the moral sense.

That is a different question entirely because it does not treat of God only, but also includes the object of His love, which, as a matter of fact, did have a real, historic beginning.

Consider a woman, a wife, who has not yet born any children. It is in her nature to love the children she may one day bear, but she does not love them as not yet conceived; they do not exist. Now suppose the woman conceives, and a child is presently growing in her womb. The child is still unknown, and yet, as the baby grows,

The Beginning of God's Love

so does the mother's love. At some point – perhaps at the first realisation that she was pregnant – her love had a beginning. The capacity to love was always there – it was in her nature – but it was only realised after the child became a real being.

Consider another example: a man and a woman who have never met. Perhaps, the woman will one day become the man's wife, but the man has no knowledge of her, and therefore, cannot love her because, for the man, it is as if she does not exist. She goes about her daily life, as he goes about his, but there is no knowledge, each of the other, and likewise, there is also no love, one of the other.

Then it happens one day, they meet by the fortunes of life, and begin an acquaintanceship, which grows into a friendship, but there is still no love. This may continue indefinitely but let us say the man does come to truly love the woman; he proves only that he has had the capacity to love all along.

But when did it begin? At some point, his love had a beginning, but in this case – in contrast with the mother in the previous example – its beginning was long after he became aware of the woman's existence.

The Purposeful Love of God

❦

Both these examples involve the sort of innate love that arises naturally. We have the capacity built-in, which can make this love seem spontaneous. At least, it is not the sort of love produced – even forced – by the effort of the will, like the love shown in the story of the good Samaritan, for instance. Though, even in that case, love is still bound to moral personality. In other words, it is from the strength of moral personality that the willing of it is possible in the first place.

But just because we have the ability native to our being does not mean it is inevitable. There are tragic examples where this innate, natural love can be suppressed, corrupted, or even denied.* Such cases show that even this native kind of love, as easy as most find it to give, is not given without the agreement and full consent of the will; that is, it is never simply the spontaneous result of nature, as it is in the animal kingdom – which holds no moral value at all.

All this is to say that the mere capacity to love does not make the act of loving inevitable. Love may be easy or hard, but it is never a passive response, even when it is given without any appreciable effort. And that is the point – it is always something given, through the positive action and consent of the will, through grace, toward its object. This means, first and foremost, it is

---

* See Rom 1:30, 2 Tim 3:3

The Beginning of God's Love

a *moral* action, which means that its character depends on the moral *personality* of the one who gives it, and therefore, it is as unique as the personality in which it is found.

It is the same for God. His love is characterised and governed by His own moral personality. He does not love by some native instinct, arbitrarily and automatically, simply because it is in His nature to love. That is to strip His love of moral personality and makes His love meaningless – I do not mean for the objects of His love, I mean meaningless for God.

If we are to treat God seriously, we must endeavour to keep the idea of a moral and personal love before us, even more than a perfect love. And the phrase, the love of God, should always be spoken with the emphasis upon God; which means, upon His *personality*. It is in this sense – of a moral and above all, a personal love – that I think it is possible to speak of a beginning of God's love for the world.

And I do not mean a beginning in a pedantic sense, as when one says the beginning of rain is when the very first water droplet falls from the sky. That is, I suppose, technically correct, but it misses the point – and it is still more wrong than it is right. Rain is what the grammarians call an uncountable noun, which, I

The Purposeful Love of God

assume, is just an extreme type of collective noun. Thus, one drop, falling by itself, does not a rain make.

I do not know how many water droplets form a quorum, and after reaching that number, it is possible to say it has begun to rain, but I venture to suggest it is a substantial number. Something less may be called a shower, but the point of this somewhat ridiculous example is that sometimes a beginning can describe an event only when it reaches a particular force of magnitude or degree.

To return to the previous example, the mother's love for her child begins when she feels the child in her womb, but as real as that love is, it pales in comparison to the love realised at the child's birth. For those who have witnessed such a thing, it is to witness a new beginning – a beginning with such force as to make everything that might have been called love before that event of no consequence, and no love at all. It is along these lines, then, that I am thinking of a beginning of God's love for the world.

Now there are two points about such a beginning that should be noted. Firstly, it is a beginning that does not arise out of sentiment or through thought alone – its foundation is in real, and therefore historic, events.

The second point follows from the first: such

The Beginning of God's Love

an event is *effectual*; that is, it is the event itself that elicits a change, not in the nature of the subject, but in the subject's disposition towards the object. There is something in that event that inspires a love, which, up to that point, is latent only and without expression.

These two points, taken together, suggest that if there is a beginning of God's love for the world, then that beginning will also coincide with actual historic events. And more importantly, those events will have real moral significance; for humanity certainly, but I mean primarily for God. Also, those events must be on an appropriate scale, which means, in this case, on the scale of the world. And this, in turn, suggests that such an event, or events, will be more or less conspicuous within history.

❦

Of course, the cross – as the supreme crisis in history – is the event that comes immediately to mind. It is also the event that necessarily holds the highest moral and personal significance for God.

However, the cross is not the beginning of God's love for the world. Yes, it has both the scale and moral gravity, but the cross is our redemption; which is more properly the beginning of God's forgiveness – it cannot be said to be the beginning of God's love. Instead, the cross *demonstrated* His love, which was already full and complete.

> "But God demonstrates His own love toward us, in that while we were yet sinners, Christ died for us."
> (Rom 5:8)

If we cast our gaze farther back in history, we find only one other event approaching the scale and moral significance required. I am thinking of the creation event, which culminated in the fashioning of man in God's own image.

That has both scale and grandeur, not to say extravagance, on God's part, and it is not unreasonable to assume the beginning of God's love for the world coincided with the creation of that world. That also seems to be the church's general assumption, as it has also been the church's experience; which is to say, the race has known, experientially, the enduring love of God down through all the ages, from its beginning to today.

But does the creation event – and the making of man in His own image – rise high enough on the moral plane? The scale of that event is certainly on the scale of the whole race, at least in a representative form through the headship of Adam. But it is unclear whether that event was high enough morally.

Could that event really become the inspiration of a love so profound that it moved God to the sacrifice of His only Son? That is the real question, and when it is put that way, surely the answer must be no – and a thousand times, no.

When the apostle says, "For God so loved the world, that He gave His only begotten Son", he is talking about something so much greater than a love born at the beginning of creation, through which, God was moved to give what He valued most – and loved more – to obtain that which He could have made again in seven days, or made many times over in seventy times seven days. No, the creation event, however glorious, was still too small a thing to inspire the sort of love demonstrated by the cross.

The cross was moral, and above all, personal – again, I do not mean for man, but for God – in a way the creative act at the beginning of the world could never be. Therefore, the beginning of God's love for the world cannot be traced back to the world's creation.

What then? Are we left to conclude that because there is nothing in all creation that can approach the value of His love, it must indeed be without a beginning? Moreover, as a love so high, so holy, and therefore, so utterly incongruous with that creation, must it be, as some theologians tell us, a love without motive or reason?

The Purposeful Love of God

Far from it! That conclusion may have a certain logic, but it leans too heavily upon the church's *experience*, which tends too quickly to a god of its own imagination. It has led to the mistaken idea that it is *only* God's nature to love, as if by some impersonal and automatic mechanism native within Godhead itself – a love that has nothing to do with His moral will and personality. That, in turn, is a love that the church has conveniently come to interpret as a love without limits, and worse, a love without conditions.

Again, those are the too-easy conclusions drawn from experience, but an experience lacking the keen sight of a faith like David's; who saw beyond his own experience, and outside time, to apprehend something of the experience of God within eternity.

If we turn our gaze in that direction, there is one other event in the history of eternity that comes into focus. It is the great wedding and marriage feast of the Lamb, and also, the destiny and hope of the saints.

The church looks forward to the final consummation of the end of the age as the realisation of her final salvation and reward. She sees it as the fulfilment of God's great redemptive plan for the restoration of the race.

But that is to see it from the perspective of the race, and the church does not often enough look towards that event from God's perspective, where it becomes the culmination of *His* work and pleasure. To be sure, it is a work that includes the final redemption of the race, but that redemption is merely prerequisite, on the way to the fashioning of something greater still – something for His own purpose and pleasure.

Just what that 'something' is, may be unclear to us at present, but its character is at least certain; it will have a character "conformed to the image of His Son".* That is no small thing, and it involves much more than simply the removal of guilt from the race, and much more even than the race made righteous. It rises higher, and must rise higher than that, if it is to elevate us to the position of brothers of the Firstborn.

Let the enormity of that sink in. If the race had never sinned and Adam had stood firm – and all his children after him – still, the race could not rise higher than the righteousness of a servant. That may be high in God's court, but it is not "the summing up of all things in Christ".†

God works towards a bride made perfect in the moral image of His beloved Son – she is the gift of holiness, offered by the Holy, unto the Holy. But that will not be realised until the end of the age, when God's work with humanity will finally be finished and made perfect. It is there, that her true character is realised

---

* Rom 8:29
† See Eph 1

and finally revealed – the hallowing, through humanity, of all that the Father values, and therefore loves most. For the bride is to be a reflection, an image, of the very *personality* of God. Now, that is something that eclipses the interest of the race, and rises to a moral significance that has real meaning to a holy God.

When we view the great wedding feast of the lamb in this light, it comes into focus with a significance scarcely to be imagined; an event of such moral magnitude that it subsumes even the crisis of the cross, with the salvation it procured, into the service of its own fulfilment, and more, it makes the cross its very surety.* It thus appropriates the moral enormity of the cross to the *means* by which it is achieved – and in the process, hallows the cross for all eternity.

Doubtless, it will not have escaped the reader that this event is also one of a work completed – like the work of the cross, it is also something finished. And as we have previously noted, this is an idea implied by the metaphor of the artisan, which shows us a love that begins, not at the beginning of his work, but at its completion – if indeed that work is beautiful in all its intended character and purpose.

---

* See Heb 7:22

The Beginning of God's Love

Again, I do not mean the creation of love itself. We need to be clear; it is the beginning of a love for the object, a love for the thing created. There is already, within the artisan, a love of the beautiful and good. That is the motivation, the rationale behind everything he makes. It is what he is passionate about, which is simply the positive expression of his personality.

But until the thing that he is fashioning is made complete, that love lacks the opportunity of expression. It abides alone, until it finds opportunity in the objects he has made.

In a similar way, humanity is the object which allows God to express His own personality – what He calls the beautiful and the good. And the love directed toward humanity is simply the passionate love of His own personality, with humanity merely the opportunity for its expression. Therefore, if one can speak of a beginning of God's love for humanity, it can only begin there, at the consummation of His great work with humanity at the end of this age.

That might not fit within a strict, hard logic, or our understanding of time, but I have not been arguing from that strict, but limited logic. Instead, I have been arguing from the *moral personality* of God.

For God, it is not time that matters, but history; by

which, I mean the thing realised, the action done. From our standpoint, that day is yet to come – it is not yet part of our experience – but it is not, because of that, outside the experience of the eternal God.

Just as the historic cross made forgiveness available to the world – regardless of whether men lived before or after that event – it is the completion of His great work in mankind, realised in the history of eternity, that is the beginning of God's love for the world.

That event became the origin, the fountainhead, of a love that fills all eternity, making His love real and actual to our experience now, even if its origin in God's eternity is yet to be enacted in the history of the race.

❧

To find the beginning of God's love for the world there, at the completion of His work, is not to say God did not love before that event, but it is to say that that event had the moral power to eclipse, and change, all that came before it in God's eternity. It became the opportunity for the expression of His love for all that He calls beautiful and good.

And far from forsaking reason, to find the beginning of God's love in the completion of His work is to discover, in that love, a rationality and motivation deep within the heart and counsel of God. Yes, it is a love unmerited, a love beyond measure, expectation or

The Beginning of God's Love

imagination, but it cannot be said to be a love without motive or reason. For God so loved the world there – at its completion and in its perfection – that He gave His only begotten Son.

The Purposeful Love of God

CHAPTER IX

THE RETURN OF THE BRIDE

IF GOD'S LOVE for the world finds its genesis at the consummation of the ages with the marriage feast of the Lamb, one would expect that focus to also be present, if not explicitly, then at least implicitly, in the life and ministry of Jesus. And that is indeed what we find, especially in Jesus' use of the wedding metaphor.

In the Old Testament, the metaphor of marriage points back to the covenant at Mt. Sinai. In the New Testament, it points to the consummation of a new covenant in the future, and so the metaphor is adapted to suit the changing focus. The image set before us now becomes that of a bridegroom and his virgin bride, rather than a husband and wife. And the dominant theme is no longer the guilt of betrayal but the joyful hope of a new beginning – the joy of a wedding and of the wedding celebration.

This change was introduced by Jesus Himself,

when, early in His ministry, He identified Himself as the bridegroom, inserting the metaphor into what was seemingly an unrelated discussion about fasting.*

He was asked, why when the Pharisees and John's disciples fasted, did His disciples not fast? His answer was that the attendants of the bridegroom cannot mourn while the bridegroom is with them, and that they would fast when the bridegroom was taken away.

He was obliquely referencing the cross that lay before Him, but there were none who heard Him that day, who could have understood what He was referring to. But that was unimportant, He was simply describing the mood of the time while He was with them, and that mood was one of joy and celebration, as of those rejoicing in the company of the bridegroom – where there is simply no place for mourning.

The metaphor probably seemed a little odd to those who heard it but He made no attempt to explain Himself further and immediately went on to suggest that, in any case, the old traditions are no longer a good fit for the new age He was ushering in.

But the fact that He employed the wedding metaphor shows His own preoccupation; it was already present and ready to His mind. In fact, it may be the only reason the metaphor found its way into His discourse that day.

It has the feel of the teacher in the company of novices, who, when answering their questions,

---

* See Matt 9:14–17

does so in a way that incorporates his own personal preoccupation – more for his own interest than their education – knowing full well they cannot possibly grasp the import of what he says.

If this was the only place we encountered the metaphor, its occurrence could probably be passed over without imputing undue significance, seeing it as nothing more than an incidental comment in service of the greater point He was making. It was undoubtedly taken as such among those who heard Him that day, but it was a theme that would recur throughout His ministry, and it is clear that His self-identification as the bridegroom held a particular, primary, and personal significance.

It is intriguing that His cousin, John, seemed to understand that better than anyone: "He who has the bride is the bridegroom; but the friend of the bridegroom, who stands and hears him, rejoices greatly because of the bridegroom's voice. So this joy of mine has been made full."*

The metaphor also appears in the parables of the

---

* Jn 3:29

wedding feast,* and in that of the ten virgins.† It was also prominent in His mind when He spoke of going to prepare a place for His disciples.‡

Furthermore, it is noteworthy that the New Testament is framed with the imagery of the wedding feast. The apostle John records the beginning of Jesus' public miracles performed at a wedding in Cana of Galilee,§ and the New Testament closes with similar imagery: "Let us rejoice and be glad and give the glory to Him, for the marriage of the Lamb has come and His bride has made herself ready."¶

Without question, it is a beautiful sentiment and the force of the metaphor, resonating through the church, has profoundly shaped the symbolism and sentiment of the Christian wedding. And if that was all there was to it, perhaps that would be enough. But none of Jesus' words were ever concerned with sentiment.

The metaphor was used by Jesus, in the preoccupation of His mind with the cross, which suggests a connection of the wedding metaphor to the fulfilment of His mission. A mission deeply informed by the prophecies contained in the Hebrew Scriptures and particularly, with respect to the metaphor, in the book

---

* Matt 22
† Matt 25
‡ Jn 14
§ Jn 2
¶ Rev 19:7

of Hosea where it is so vividly portrayed.

But Hosea's story remained incomplete. It had never reached closure, having arrived at its end with only a partial reconciliation at best. It had left Israel with a lingering malaise, guilt, and sense of loss. And to the extent that Israel could have any hope of a full restoration at all, it had remained in the nation's consciousness as an uncertain hope, a *probationary* hope. And in any case, it was a hope that would not be realised, if at all, "for many days".*

It was into this uneasy melancholy, after many days, that Jesus appeared to Israel, announcing to anyone who could understand, that the story told through Hosea had now been taken up again. For the metaphor of the bridegroom that Jesus introduced was none other than the continuation of that same redemptive story found in the book of Hosea. To Jesus, it was simply another way – and one that meant more to Himself personally, than to anyone else – of announcing that the kingdom of God was at hand.

It is true, it was not the continuation that anyone expected – certainly not what the religious rulers expected – for it came veiled behind the paradox of a

---

* Hos 3:4

new bride and a new beginning; that much the Jewish leaders did understand. They saw clearly enough, as they thought, that Christ's message was a break from the past and therefore no continuation at all. And to some extent, the church has shared their understanding; after all, Christ had come to make all things new.* The Jewish leaders understood that, and were incensed by it.

Whatever the Jews had learned from the sin offering, they knew that the grain offering was a memorial before God; that is, they knew that God does not forget. That has been their sorrow, but also their comfort, down through the ages – and the hope they cling to still, because it meant their suffering, in the end, would not be for nothing. God would remember His people before the end, and Israel would be restored.

That meant continuity, and it meant forgiveness; it did not mean the beginning of a new story – not even forgiveness can do that. If forgiveness can remove the guilt written in history, it cannot un-write history itself. Therefore, there could be no new beginning, which meant all their long, failed history, would continue to haunt them like an uneasy dream in the shadow of their collective consciousness – and how could it be otherwise.

---

* Rev 21:5

The Return of the Bride

❦

So, it can seem, on the face of it, as if we have two different stories set before us, with the new story introduced by Jesus to contrast with the first – two novels on the same theme perhaps, and even from the same author, but two different books nonetheless.

The first was a fine attempt to be sure, but it failed in many respects – and finally at the end. It began well enough, and with a grand gesture. The heroin was beautiful and so full of promise, if only she had the strength to realise it. But she stumbled, and in the end her beauty corrupted and ruined her. And though our hero was faithful, his faithfulness served only to add to the sense of tragedy for them both.

Yes, there was something of an uneasy reconciliation toward the end, even forgiveness, but inevitably, as with all the great tragedies, it was too little and too late – it had a history which could not be undone.

So, it seems the only solution left for us is to close the pages of the book, though we have not quite reached the end of the story, put it back on the shelf, and reach for another – one without the baggage of a ruined past – in the hope that a new story, a better story, will help us forget the first. For in our hearts, that is what we really seek; it is easier to start over, it is so much easier to forget.

Into this national malaise, Jesus appears, introducing

a new story and a new bride, set in a different time and a better place. Coming down from heaven, she is exceedingly beautiful and full of grace, but she wears her beauty lightly like the morning dew on the fragile apple blossom, and she is not overcome. She is innocent as the first day, and she is worthy – yes, worthy – and the angels gasp as they behold her beauty, refracted through liquid diamonds in the golden light of the morning sun...

And thus, a new, and a better story begins, or so it seems, and the Jewish leaders baulked at it; understanding that a new beginning meant the sweeping aside of all that came before. At least, that was their sense from Jesus' message; and it was not lost on them that they were the ones to be swept aside.

It ran counter to all they thought they knew. It was an affront to their indomitable national hope for the fulfilment of all the glorious promises to Israel, and of their trust in Israel's God – and not least, a mortal wound to their national pride.

But mostly, it was simply beyond their imagination that these two stories could actually be the opening and closing chapters of the same book; that the protagonists were one and the same. It could not possibly be true, because if it were true, that would mean the story paradoxically ends at the beginning. And not by a path circular in course, by which we end up where we had first begun. The ending here, has no sense of a return to paradise lost; rather, it moves forward to a more glorious consummation, through the deliberate execution and determination of history. But that would mean that our story begins with ruin, and it ends, not merely in restoration but in innocence; it starts with something broken and yet it ends, not with something mended but with something *never* broken – something made perfect.

If the Jewish leaders understood the absurdity, Jesus never saw it so. He did not come to abolish the law but to fulfil it, but He saw His mission from a different perspective, as one who knew history from its beginning to end, and especially its end, and therefore, as one who could make sense of all that long history in between and understand its purpose.

That purpose was to call out a bride from within humanity; a bride who was no more inclusive of the whole nation of Israel than of the whole race. But because of the promises made to Abraham and David, He first made His appeal to the Jewish nation. Concerning the prophecies of Hosea, He was saying to the nation, "your story, your *history*, continues with Me".

It was a story that would lead Him through the cross but, even as He walked deliberately into that darkness,

His eyes were fixed on the joy that was set before Him on the other side; beyond the cross certainly, but also beyond the resurrection, toward the joy of the final realisation of all that the Father had been fashioning for Him since the world began.

And its completion would be marked by the glorious and joyful marriage feast of the Lamb and His bride. This was the joy set before Him, for which He endured the cross, not merely for the restoration of our faith, but for its perfecting.* It was because Christ could see the end of that history that He spoke of a wedding, and a bride, always in terms of joy and celebration.

Now, the church has been sympathetic to the Jewish sentiment, with its sense of failure and wretchedness. We understand we are but grafted onto the original vine, and our histories intersect and combine with theirs; our sin and guilt are one and the same. And if, in this life, our sins may be forgiven, yet we nevertheless live out our lives with the resulting consequences and loss.

Thus, we know that history has not been erased, and as if in an effort not to be outdone, or to prove a more righteous humility, we pronounce a continual judgment upon ourselves. We take up Isaiah's lament, that "we are

---

*   Heb 12:2

all like an unclean thing, and all our righteousnesses are like filthy rags".* Or as one theologian has represented God as saying; "Your sins have made you disgustingly ugly. But I love you anyway, not because you are attractive, but because *it is my nature to love.*"†

This representation of His love may have the appearance of elevating it to some higher plane, but it does so by removing God from His throne, and crowning love in His place, which in the end, makes love meaningless – again, I do not mean meaningless for man but utterly meaningless for God.

For if God loves without regard to His own personality, without regard to what *He* calls beautiful and holy, it empties love of all that makes it His, because it empties it of Himself. It ceases to be personal and therefore, perhaps worst of all, it empties that love of the possibility of joy – the very thing that was so prominent in the mind of Christ.

But Christ never saw His bride that way. He did not come to salvage from the wreckage, the little that could still be of some heavenly use. He did not see Himself as one last, and desperate, attempt, at the saving of a grand project ill-conceived and in need of a radical overhaul. And He certainly did not lower His expectations to the

---

* Is 64:6 (NKJV)

† The Difficult Doctrine of the Love of God, p71, D.A. Carson, emphasis added. D.A. Carson is a Christian writer for whom I have a great deal of respect. However, on this point I must respectfully disagree.

accommodation of a bride who was – if I may be blunt – damaged goods.

There is no sense in which the joy set before Him was merely making the best of such an unfortunate situation as having to spend eternity with a bride so plain and unbecoming, and so incommensurate with Himself. On the contrary, Christ came for a bride made beautiful, spotless and perfect, where the force of those words lies equally in 'made'. Made perfect; that is, fashioned with deliberate intent and skill.

Which means there is in His sacrifice, a design and intent that goes beyond the pragmatic need of the race, and reaches to the eternal hallowing of His own holy Name. And it does so, not by erasing the history of the race, but by subsuming it to His eternal purpose and joy – where it becomes the power of God in a work so utterly complete, and perfect, that even our need to forget is transformed into the need to remember; where the scars in His glorified hands become a memorial, not to our shame but to the undying glory of the purposeful love of God.

It never was His purpose to wipe away history as an experiment in free-will gone wrong, an affront to the perfection of God. He has purposed to use that history, after the counsel of His will, to fashion a more perfect work for Himself; a work which without that history would not be complete, perfect.

The frail and flawed history of the race, every minute of it, far from being an unfortunate and unplanned catastrophe on God's part, is rather an integral part of the process the great Artisan has purposed, in holy love, to fashion a people into a work that is beautiful, good, and perfect for Himself.

From our perspective, the race's history is an obstacle to that end, but it is the glory of God to ordain and use it for His own purpose. Therefore, He can say with a matter-of-factness and simplicity:

> "Come now, and let us reason together,"
> Says the LORD,
> "Though your sins are as scarlet,
> They will be as white as snow."
> (Is 1:18a)

Christ came in the love, and the passion of that work, and with the quiet confidence of its fulfilment. It was the *realisation* of that work that was the joy set before Him.

He came to save, certainly, but the redemption He accomplished was part of a deliberate work of God, in the fashioning of a bride who is worthy. I do not mean with regard to herself, I mean worthy for God. We must learn to see everything more from God's perspective;

to understand the bride as a work *of* God, *by* God, and *for* God.

And therefore, her worth is not to be diminished for the sake of the humility of the race, but rather to be raised to the glory and honour of His Name, because it is the honour of God that matters most, even more than the humbling of the pride of man. To see His bride as worthy is not an affront to the holiness of God; it is *required* by that holiness.*

Viewing the work of God from His perspective, it is not hard to understand that completed work must necessarily be worthy. However, what is harder to see is that it is a *moral* work, and therefore, it demands an equally active *moral response* on the part of the race – not unto salvation, but unto the perfecting of that work. And therefore, to that end, circumstances must be created to give the opportunity for the free exercise of that moral response.

To return to the story of Hosea and Gomer, we can see it included ransom, deliverance from sin, and forgiveness. That was all done for Gomer unilaterally and without her consent, but even so, it was not complete. It lacked the positive and active moral response, on the

---

* Heb 12:14

The Return of the Bride

part of Gomer, that would make it complete.

Which is why, when Jesus took up that story once more with the preaching of His gospel, it was a gospel that demanded a response from those who heard it.

It is no coincidence that both John and Jesus understood their ministries in connection with the metaphor of marriage, and that both also came preaching a baptism of repentance. The repentance they were calling for was not simply a turning away from sin, but it was, firstly, the positive turning towards God, with one's whole moral personality.

And their message was delivered with urgency, because they both understood that the time of probation, prophesied through Hosea, was about to close, and the hour of decision was upon the nation at last; and upon each individual who made up the nation.

There was nothing inevitable or automatic about their inclusion in His great work – and by extension, His love. Their inclusion must be actively sought for on their part, through the positive, moral action of the will.

That element of decision was there by design, and it was not something that could be ignored without consequence. It went to the very heart of each and every individual moral personality. A decision *must* be made, one way or the other – it was a moral imperative.

Or, to put it as Jesus did when He was talking with the Samaritan woman at the well, "an hour is coming, and now is, when the true worshipers will worship the

Father in spirit and truth; for such people the Father seeks to be His worshipers."*

And it is not without significance that Jesus made that statement after His conversation with the Samaritan woman had once again turned to the subject of marriage.

---

* Jn 4:23

CHAPTER X

THE MORAL IMPERATIVE

OR THE CHILD, moral authority is purely an external matter but that does not mean it is particularly objective. Certainly, all authority is imposed upon the child by an external agency but, whether it be a law of government or of God, the child experiences that external authority solely through the parent.

From the point of view of the child, there is no distinction between the parent and the authority they project – the parent is the authority. Thus, in the small world of the child, authority is completely bound up with the identity of the parent. When the child disobeys, it is not an objective law that is broken; it is the *parent* that has been wronged, which, for the child, makes the idea of authority intensely personal.

It is, in fact, a stage of life for the child that comes very close to how we should see our relation to God's laws. It is surely part of the reason Jesus said we cannot enter the kingdom of God unless we become like children; for with children, everything is personal.

But a child's understanding of authority changes as they grow. Gradually, the child comes to see the parent as someone also under authority, and that authority, as something external and independent from the identity of the parent. As time goes on, external authorities in the child's life multiply, and the vast majority of those originate with, or are mediated through, impersonal agencies. Thus, in the mind of the child, the connection between authority and personality begins to fragment and fade – though never completely.

As the child becomes more aware of the parent as a person in their own right – with an identity beyond the parental role – the child can see there are some authorities that remain bound to the parent's own identity. Though the child now recognises that the source of that authority exists independently, and does not originate with the parent, the force of that external authority seems strangely redundant for the parent because it has somehow become the parent's own; it has been subsumed to the parent's own moral personality and now operates as if it were their own. It is, therefore, no longer something to be obeyed because, by the free action of the parent's will, it has now become their own ruling principle.

That may sound strange at first, but it is a process that is repeated, to varying degrees, in virtually every one of us, resulting in a moral autonomy in many areas of our lives. It represents an ideal that we are all called to.

Every good parent knows this instinctively, for it is the hope of the parent that the values they teach their children will one day be internalised; that is, it is the parent's desire that the external, objective authority, that has hitherto been the sole foundation of the child's moral authority – their ruling principle – is in due course replaced by an immanent and autonomous authority; an authority that is self-determined and results in the child's own self-governance. When that eventually happens, we say they have become their own person.

But moral autonomy comes with responsibility, and if it is an important step toward maturity, it is not an end in itself, it must be coupled with good moral character; without which, moral autonomy becomes a dangerous force directed toward selfish and often wicked ends – to the destruction of much, and harm of many.

In that case, for society's sake and also for the individual's, their moral autonomy must be abrogated, and the individual ruled once more by an external authority – with a consequent loss of freedom. Thus, even in civil society, this idea of moral autonomy is recognised as both a privilege and a responsibility, which can only be trusted to those of sufficient character.

It is this idea of moral autonomy, quite as much as character, that is at the heart of what it means to be mature, or as the writers of the New Testament are want to say, to be perfect.

In the New Testament, to be perfect means to be *complete*, in a moral sense, which is something beyond the mere absence of sin. That is a modern mischaracterisation based upon logic that lacks the moral dimension. The New Testament authors were not talking about an impersonal, objective sinlessness; they urged us to be perfect despite our sin.

If a simple sinlessness was chiefly what God required, righteousness could have been achieved for the race by a much easier and more direct path. It could have been woven into the nature of man from the very beginning; not so crudely as to render it robotic, perhaps, but in a more artful way more akin to an instinct. But even that kind of righteousness, though sinless, would not have been perfect because it lacks moral autonomy; by which, I mean it would not have been chosen.

But God requires a *moral* perfection, which means righteousness to be sure, but righteousness desired and chosen for its own sake – by the free and full confession of our own moral wills. We must be holy as He is holy,* but we must *choose* to be holy. Which is to say, His holiness must become our own ruling principle, operating out of

---

*   1 Pet 1:16

our own moral autonomy. Simple, pragmatic obedience is not enough; that may be even more offensive to a holy God than a free and hearty rebellion, and it may incur a judgement all the more severe.

Again, we see God's desire for this moral maturity, or perfection, in the story of Gomer. For it is evident that her story is something more than a call to mere sinless obedience. It is a call to more even, than faithful relationship – though that is included in it. Rather, it is a call to a moral perfection, whereby Gomer, without compulsion, and of her own free will and desire, *chooses* the good.

When Gomer had transgressed almost to the point of self-destruction, God intervened through the action of Hosea, who ransomed her to himself. But it was not a full restoration. She had lost the privilege of self-governance; her moral autonomy had been stripped from her and she was now under the external and enforced authority of her master. If Hosea was still, technically, her husband, that relationship was now secondary to Hosea's lordship. Under compulsion of that lordship, her righteousness was not truly her own, but merely a practical sinlessness.

Further, Hosea's lordship over Gomer was probationary in nature, its duration extended by grace, but still limited in time. Implicit in that probation was either the full restoration, or the dissolution, of the marriage relationship – along with the love that accompanied it – and it would be Gomer's response that would determine which would prevail. Hosea was waiting for something from Gomer; some change on her part that was required for his own sake but, unlike a pragmatic obedience, it must be chosen freely, with her whole heart and moral will.

※

And concerning his love, perhaps the reader thinks I have gone too far to suggest Hosea's love might be withdrawn from her. From a certain point of view, i.e., Gomer's, it does indeed appear that Hosea's love was unaffected by her treachery, that there was nothing she could do that would extinguish or lessen it in the slightest degree. His love seemed only to grow with time – in spite of the worst she had done. It must have seemed to Gomer to be a love of the sort that the church today naïvely calls 'unconditional'.

But if there was nothing that Gomer had done up to that point that had caused his love to be withdrawn, that did not mean his love was unconditional – it simply meant it was patient and forbearing up to that point; unlimited in its capacity perhaps, but not necessarily by time.

She had confused pity for weakness, and had

The Moral Imperative

misjudged the quality, and even more, the source of his love. In her conceit, it was too easy to believe his love was centred in her; an infatuation compelled by her own beauty and worth. But if Hosea saw any worth in Gomer, it was not to be found in who she was but in who she might become. If Gomer was caught in the gaze of Hosea's love – if it looked in her direction – it was yet focused on something beyond her.

Its source and centre were to be found within the character of the prophet himself – in his desire to realise something greater than them both; something beautiful and good. It was the possibility, and more, the hope, of seeing that good realised in Gomer that inspired his love. That is where its true focus lay. Indeed, if there is one aspect regarding Hosea's love for Gomer that stands out above all else, it is that it is strangely *independent* from her. But independent does not mean unconditional, and the two should not be conflated.

The ancient Greeks had a word for this kind of love: they called it *eros*. It was a love that originated within the subject, and as such, its passion and motivation was bound up within the moral character of the one loving. And because its genesis was there, it could manifest both the highest, as well as the basest forms of love.

If the character of an individual was profane, *eros*

simply became a reflection of that same character; where it rose no higher than lust – as self-serving and as transient as the person from whom it sprung. However, if it was born of noble character, it was possible for that love to rise to the very highest, and most sublime quality, because its passion was on a higher moral plane; and the love it produced was equal to it.

It is with just such a love we are dealing with here: a passionate love, but of the highest moral quality. And though it was turned in her direction, its passion was focused on something beyond her, something she could become part of if she wished, though not by default; certainly not by a mere pragmatic obedience or submission. It must be sought for its own sake, through the active, positive, and genuine desire of her own moral will.

In light of this comes a warning because, if Hosea's love was a moral love, it was also sustained, not by sentiment, but by the moral power of the will. And if it is the will that sustains it, then it is also possible, by the action of that same moral will, for love to be withdrawn if its desire and purpose is at last denied.*

His purpose and desire, his passion, was for the

---

* See Hos 9:15

The Moral Imperative

beautiful and the good. That might include Gomer but, regardless of her participation in it or not, it would endure nonetheless, because it was *independent* of her. His love would endure, but not necessarily upon Gomer, for her fate was bound up with her own moral choices.

Therefore, while Hosea's love was turned towards her, it became more than an invitation; it became a moral imperative that she make his passion her own. It was not enough that she simply recognise the good, it was not enough that her behaviour was constrained by the good; she must become part of it. It must, of her own free desire, be subsumed to her own moral personality; it must truly become her own ruling principle.

Mere righteousness was not enough, her righteousness must spring freely from her own moral autonomy; that is, her righteousness must be a mature righteousness – it must be complete, perfect. Only then could she realise within herself the good and the beautiful, and finally become who she was always meant to be – for in Hebrew, Gomer simply means complete, perfect.

Humanity is in the same position as Gomer. It abides, for now, under the patient love of God but His love is not gratuitous; it is not irrational or without motivation. It is a love centred within His own holy personality, which means, first and foremost, it is a *moral* love – ruled, not by sentiment but by the passion of His own holy will.

And it is His will to see that same passion realised in humanity; and it will be realized, with or without our individual participation. Therefore, His desire becomes, for each unique individual, much more than a sentimental hope, or aspiration. It becomes a demand for moral perfection, a demand for the holy – the holiness, without which no one will see God.*

It is too quickly assumed that that high standard of holiness is met and fulfilled by a sinless humanity; that mere sinlessness was the end Christ died to achieve. But that sinlessness is only a by-product of what He is fashioning from humanity – and it is not the greater, or the hardest, part.

God demands from the race, for His own sake, something greater than a mere practical sinlessness, something more even, than a compelled righteousness; He demands moral perfection, in the sense I have described. Which means a righteousness in harmony with Himself, a righteousness that springs freely from our own moral autonomy, which does not need to be

---

* See Heb 12:14

taught and has no need of any external authority – even God's authority.

That is a terrifying thought, for who is there who does not recognise the impossibility of such a demand? And yet it stands nevertheless, as a moral imperative for the entire race. Our entrance into God's kingdom and His fellowship is conditional upon it.

But if there is no hope for the weakness of man, there is hope in the power of God. He is not without the moral power to realise His own purpose and desire. He is *the* Artisan, and we are His workmanship. And He works with us still, and what He has purposed, what He is fashioning, He will also achieve and realise by His own skill and moral power.*

The sacrifice of Christ was not for sin alone. That was necessary, but in itself, it was not the thing pleasing to God. More than the bearing of our guilt – and with it the bearing away of God's wrath – was the offering of something greater still. It was something greater even than mere obedience; though that is something the church today needs to press more fully. For the confession of full obedience is more to God than the confession of sin and the removal of guilt.

---

* See Phil 1:6

The Purposeful Love of God

But those are the outward expressions and consequence of a holy obedience from the heart; by which, I mean the offering of His whole Personality in the passion of His love for all that the Father calls beautiful and good; offered back to God by Christ, for His own sake first, and then on behalf of the race.

That is the thing pleasing to God, that is the real satisfaction of God in the obedience of the cross; that all those who are in Christ might become the righteousness of God by our inclusion in Him, "just as He chose us *in Him* before the foundation of the world, that we should be holy and blameless before Him in love."*

Thus, He says:

> "I will put my law within them and on their heart I will write it... they will not teach again, each man his neighbor and each man his brother, saying, 'Know the LORD', for they will all know Me, from the least of them to the greatest of them."
>
> (Jer 31:33–34)

That is what it means to be 'in Christ'. But however that transformation is achieved by God in the metaphysical, it does not mean the destruction of our own identity and our transformation into robots. For that would be the negation of the very thing He seeks to create, and therefore, He will not write His law on our

---

* Eph 1:4, emphasis added.

hearts, except at our own invitation and consent.

✥

That is no limitation on God, whereby the creature can exercise power over God and hold His own love to ransom, in order to secure our entrance into His kingdom. His love is His own, and it does not compel Him against His own holy will.

The gift of our free will does not mitigate, or negate, the sovereignty of God; it is by His sovereign decree that He has given it – whether we want it or not. Our moral freedom to choose is a *means* to God's own end; it serves *His* purpose, and for His own satisfaction and joy.

The issue has never been whether man has free will, on the one hand, or whether everything is predestined, on the other. Rather, it is that God has predestined, in Christ, that only those who choose the good freely – with their whole moral personality, in spirit and truth – shall share in His life and enter into the kingdom He has prepared for them.

Our moral freedom is no license to do as we please, without consequences to ourselves. He has made that abundantly clear.

> "I have set before you life and death,
> the blessing and the curse. So choose life."
> (Deut 30:19)

The Purposeful Love of God

Our participation in His life is offered freely – if we choose it. But to choose life is not simply to choose to exist, without regard to His moral personality. It is to choose life on His terms; that is, to choose *His* life – life in His Spirit and in His holiness. Thus, to choose life is to choose *Him*, His whole personality, which includes all that He calls beautiful and good.

And the choice must be made whole, because only those who truly love what He loves, what I have called the beautiful and the good – which means for God, the holy – will love Him in spirit and truth. He seeks these exclusively and it is, ultimately, only on these that His love will continue to abide.

All this is to recognise that God's love for the world does not exist independently from His moral purposes for mankind. His love towards humanity is the *fruit* of the realisation of those purposes and, therefore, God's love is not something to be taken for granted or presumed upon; it is not unconditional or without end for those who turn their backs on His call.

Now, for a time, as if on probation, the race abides under the love of God, as it is turned in our direction – even as its desire is focused upon something greater in each of us. And He now waits, as for Gomer, to see if we

The Moral Imperative

will choose to be mature, and made perfect.

"Let us rejoice and be glad and give the glory to Him, for the marriage of the Lamb has come and His bride has made herself ready."
(Rev 19:7)